SPIES, SCOUTS AND RAIDERS

Irregular Operations

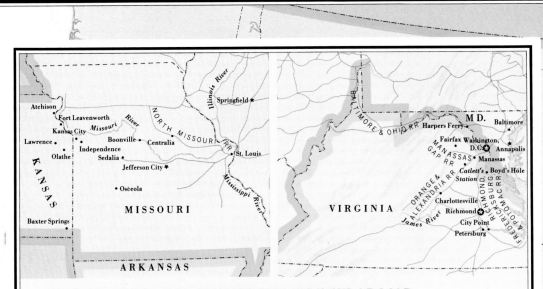

THE CONTESTED REGIONS OF THE IRREGULAR WAR

While the armies of the Union and the Confederacy clashed on scores of battlefields, a second, clandestine war was being waged throughout the land. Across the rolling landscape of northern Virginia moved bands of Confederate partisans and raiders who struck at Union camps and railroads and then melted back into the countryside. Spies, scouts and saboteurs moved by night along Virginia's rivers — to observe enemy troop movements and to infiltrate the very capitals of the Union and the Confederacy.

In western Virginia, the Allegheny Mountains were home to marauding bands of hill people who descended from forest hideouts to stage raids and disappear. The stark landscapes of Kansas and Missouri supported a harsher kind of guerrilla war conducted by men whose commitment to killing and plundering seemed as strong as their loyalty to a flag.

The irregular warfare that flickered and flared like a brush fire across these vast spaces involved scores of men and a handful of women. At their worst they were simple bandits and at their best they were living legends, incarnating the causes for which they fought and served. The most famous of them even put his name on four counties of Virginia farmland, a region known to friend and foe alike as Mosby's Confederacy.

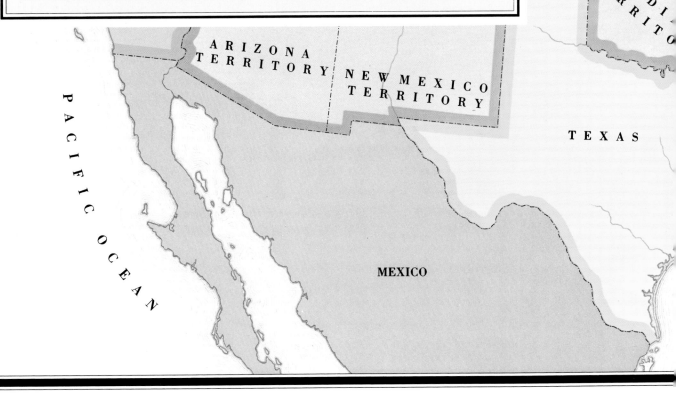

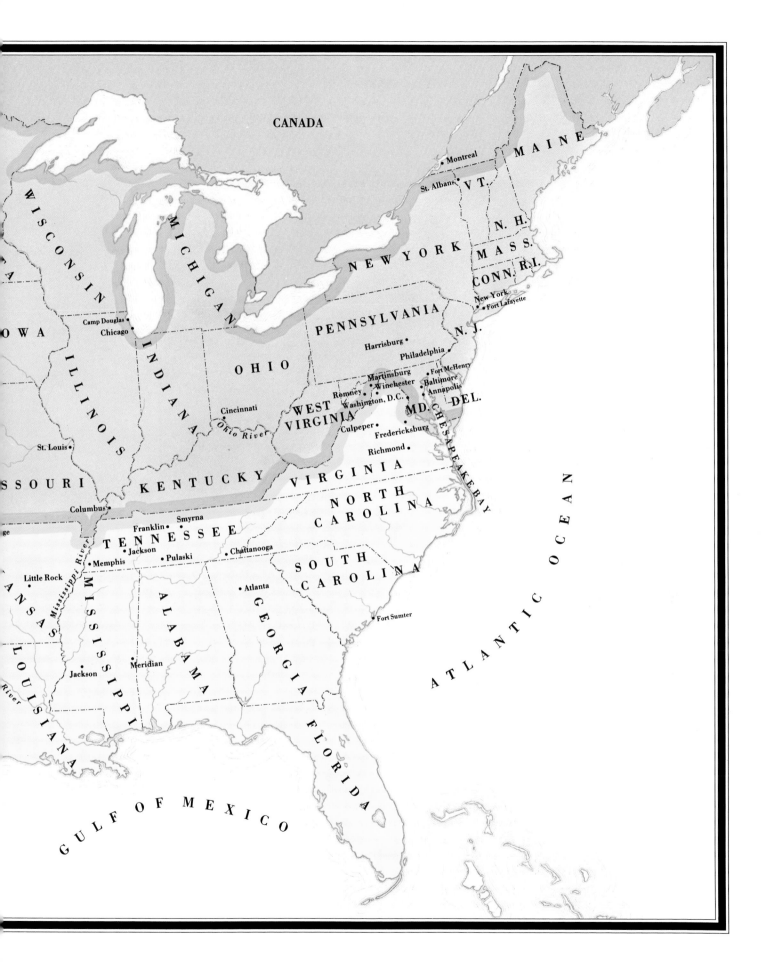

Other Publications:

UNDERSTANDING COMPUTERS
THE ENCHANTED WORLD
YOUR HOME
THE KODAK LIBRARY OF CREATIVE PHOTOGRAPHY
GREAT MEALS IN MINUTES
PLANET EARTH
COLLECTOR'S LIBRARY OF THE CIVIL WAR
THE EPIC OF FLIGHT
THE GOOD COOK
THE SEAFARERS
WORLD WAR II
HOME REPAIR AND IMPROVEMENT
THE OLD WEST

For information on and a full description of any of the
Time-Life Books series listed above, please write:
Reader Information, Time-Life Books
541 North Fairbanks Court, Chicago, Illinois 60611

This volume is one of a series that chronicles in full the
events of the American Civil War, 1861-1865.
Other books in the series include:
Brother against Brother: The War Begins
First Blood: Fort Sumter to Bull Run
The Blockade: Runners and Raiders
The Road to Shiloh: Early Battles in the West
Forward to Richmond: McClellan's Peninsular Campaign
Decoying the Yanks: Jackson's Valley Campaign
Confederate Ordeal: The Southern Home Front
Lee Takes Command: From Seven Days to Second Bull Run
The Coastal War: Chesapeake Bay to Rio Grande
Tenting Tonight: The Soldier's Life
The Bloodiest Day: The Battle of Antietam
War on the Mississippi: Grant's Vicksburg Campaign
Rebels Resurgent: Fredericksburg to Chancellorsville
Twenty Million Yankees: The Northern Home Front
Gettysburg: The Confederate High Tide
The Struggle for Tennessee: Tupelo to Stones River
The Fight for Chattanooga: Chickamauga to Missionary Ridge

The Cover: Peering through a screen of cattails,
Confederate guerrillas draw a bead on their foe in a
painting by Tennessee artist Gilbert Gaul. Such
furtive assaults by irregular troops plagued the Federal Army as it moved through the South, forcing
the diversion of thousands of men from the battle-
fronts to protect the vulnerable Union rear.

THE CIVIL WAR

SPIES, SCOUTS AND RAIDERS

BY

THE EDITORS

OF

TIME-LIFE BOOKS

Irregular Operations

TIME-LIFE BOOKS, ALEXANDRIA, VIRGINIA

Time-Life Books Inc.
is a wholly owned subsidiary of
TIME INCORPORATED

FOUNDER: Henry R. Luce 1898-1967

Editor-in-Chief: Henry Anatole Grunwald
President: J. Richard Munro
Chairman of the Board: Ralph P. Davidson
Corporate Editor: Jason McManus
Group Vice President, Books: Reginald K. Brack Jr.
Vice President, Books: George Artandi

TIME-LIFE BOOKS INC.

EDITOR: George Constable
Executive Editor: George Daniels
Editorial General Manager: Neal Goff
Director of Design: Louis Klein
Editorial Board: Dale M. Brown, Roberta Conlan,
Ellen Phillips, Gerry Schremp, Donia Ann Steele,
Rosalind Stubenberg, Kit van Tulleken,
Henry Woodhead
Director of Research: Phyllis K. Wise
Director of Photography: John Conrad Weiser

PRESIDENT: William J. Henry
Senior Vice President: Christopher T. Linen
Vice Presidents: Stephen L. Bair, Edward Brash,
Robert A. Ellis, John M. Fahey Jr., Juanita T. James,
James L. Mercer, Wilhelm R. Saake, Paul R. Stewart,
Leopoldo Toralballa

The Civil War
Series Director: Henry Woodhead
Designer: Cynthia T. Richardson
Series Administrator: Philip Brandt George

Editorial Staff for *Spies, Scouts and Raiders*
Associate Editors: Jane A. Martin (text), Jeremy Ross
(pictures)
Staff Writers: Thomas H. Flaherty Jr.,
Stephen G. Hyslop, R. W. Murphy,
Daniel Stashower, David S. Thomson
Researchers: Susan V. Kelly, Mark Moss
Copy Coordinator: Jayne E. Rohrich
Picture Coordinator: Betty H. Weatherley
Editorial Assistant: Donna Fountain
Special Contributors: Champ Clark, William C. Davis,
Feroline Burrage Higginson, Wendy Buehr Murphy

Editorial Operations
Design: Ellen Robling (assistant director)
Copy Chief: Diane Ullius
Editorial Operations: Caroline A. Boubin (manager)
Production: Celia Beattie
Quality Control: James J. Cox (director)
Library: Louise D. Forstall

Correspondents: Elisabeth Kraemer-Singh (Bonn);
Margot Hapgood, Dorothy Bacon (London); Miriam
Hsia (New York); Maria Vincenza Aloisi, Josephine du
Brusle (Paris); Ann Natanson (Rome). Valuable
assistance was also provided by: Carolyn Chubet
(New York).

The Consultants:
Colonel John R. Elting, USA (Ret.), a former Associate
Professor at West Point, is the author of *Battles for Scandi-
navia* in the Time-Life Books World War II series and of
*The Battle of Bunker's Hill, The Battles of Saratoga, Mili-
tary History and Atlas of the Napoleonic Wars, American
Army Life,* and *The Superstrategist.* Co-author of *A
Dictionary of Soldier Talk,* he is also editor of the three
volumes of *Military Uniforms in America, 1755-1867,* and
associate editor of *The West Point Atlas of American Wars.*

William A. Frassanito, a Civil War historian and lecturer
specializing in photograph analysis, is the author of two
award-winning studies, *Gettysburg: A Journey in Time* and
*Antietam: The Photographic Legacy of America's Bloodiest
Day,* and a companion volume, *Grant and Lee, The Virginia Campaigns.* He has also served as chief consultant to the
photographic history series *The Image of War.*

Les Jensen, Director of the Second Armored Division
Museum, Fort Hood, Texas, specializes in Civil War arti-
facts and is a conservator of historic flags. He is a contribu-
tor to *The Image of War* series, consultant for numerous
Civil War publications and museums, and a member of
the Company of Military Historians. He was formerly Curator of the U.S. Army Transportation Museum at Fort
Eustis, Virginia, and before that Curator of the Museum
of the Confederacy in Richmond, Virginia.

Michael McAfee specializes in military uniforms and has
been Curator of Uniforms and History at the West Point
Museum since 1970. A fellow of the Company of Military
Historians, he coedited with Colonel Elting *Long Endure:
The Civil War Years,* and he collaborated with Frederick
Todd on *American Military Equipage.* He is the author of
Artillery of the American Revolution, 1775-1783, and has
written numerous articles for *Military Images Magazine.*

James P. Shenton, Professor of History at Columbia University, is a specialist in 19th Century American political
and social history, with particular emphasis on the Civil
War period. He is the author of *Robert John Walker* and
Reconstruction South.

Library of Congress Cataloguing in Publication Data
Main entry under title:
Spies, scouts, and raiders.
(The Civil War)
Bibliography: p.
Includes index.
1. United States — History — Civil War, 1861-1865 —
Secret service. 2. United States — History — Civil War,
1861-1865 — Scouts and scouting. 3. Guerrillas — United
States — History — 19th century. 4. United States —
History — Civil War, 1861-1865 — Commando
operations.
I. Time-Life Books. II. Title. III. Series.
E608.D29 1986   973.7'85   85-21014
ISBN 0-8094-4716-9
ISBN 0-8094-4713-4 (lib. bdg.)

CONTENTS

Currents of Conspiracy

"It is beyond a doubt that from some source the rebels have received early, and to them, valuable notice of the intended actions of the government."

ALLAN PINKERTON, FEDERAL COUNTERESPIONAGE CHIEF, AFTER THE BATTLE OF BULL RUN, JULY 27, 1862

Shortly before 6 p.m. on February 22, 1861, the President-elect of the United States was supping in the dining room of the Jones House in Harrisburg, Pennsylvania, when, by prearrangement, he was called away from the table. After going up to his room, Abraham Lincoln changed from dinner dress into a traveling suit, put on an overcoat, stuffed a soft, slouch hat into its pocket and, with a shawl folded over his arm, hastily departed the hotel.

In the gathering darkness Lincoln was taken by carriage to a Pennsylvania Railroad siding where awaited a locomotive, its steam already up, and a single, empty passenger car. Boarding with Lincoln was a large and muscular man named Ward Hill Lamon, an Illinois lawyer who had ridden the circuit with Honest Abe. Slated to become U.S. Marshal for the District of Columbia in the new Administration, Lamon had meanwhile nominated himself as Lincoln's personal bodyguard. In that capacity he carried not only his own ham-size fists but an arsenal comprising four pistols of varying dimensions; two large, sharp knives; a blackjack; and a pair of brass knuckles.

For the first leg of the trip that followed, the railroad tracks to Philadelphia had been cleared of traffic. Moreover, lest persons unfriendly to the Union might, despite all precautions, notice Lincoln's leave-taking and try to send word that the President-elect was on the move, all telegraph lines from Harrisburg had been cut.

Arriving in Philadelphia shortly after 10 p.m., Lincoln and Lamon were met and whisked into a carriage by a stocky, hard-eyed man with a close-trimmed beard and a plug hat perched atop his head. He was Allan Pinkerton, founder and operator of a private detective agency in Chicago, now on a special assignment. With Pinkerton in charge, Lincoln was driven from the Pennsylvania Railroad Station to the depot of the Philadelphia, Wilmington & Baltimore Railroad. There he was spirited as quickly and quietly as possible aboard the last car of the regular night train for Baltimore, where it would make a connection for Washington.

The rear half of the sleeper, sequestered from the rest of the car by a drawn curtain, had been reserved by one of Pinkerton's operatives — a Mrs. Kate Warne — to accommodate her "invalid brother," who retired almost immediately to the sanctuary of his berth. Lamon, Pinkerton, Kate Warne and two other bodyguards were now aboard and bristling with weaponry; around midnight the train moved into the darkness, carrying Abraham Lincoln toward the nation's capital where, only 10 days hence, he would solemnly swear to preserve, protect and defend the Constitution of the United States.

Still seven weeks away was the confrontation at Fort Sumter that would signal the start of the Civil War. Yet Lincoln's clandestine journey signified the fact that a secret war had already begun. Now embryonic, it

President Lincoln confers with spy chief Allan Pinkerton *(left)* during an inspection trip of the Antietam battlefield with General John McClernand *(right)* in 1862.

would soon take deadly shape as a contest of spies and counterspies; of saboteurs who took extraordinary risks in their efforts to destroy enemy property; of iron-nerved scouts who mingled with enemy soldiers in enemy camps; of raiders who swooped deep into hostile territory to spread destruction or terror; of ghostly partisans so numerous and so disruptive that they could divert large bodies of regular troops from their normal duties; and of bushwhackers who killed and looted simply for the lust of it.

These were the irregulars of the Civil War, and they were as motley a lot as ever existed — patriots and renegades, martyrs and traitors, heroes and rascals, idealists and fortune-seekers, bureaucrats and lone wolves. They included creatures of the dark and those who sought the glare of notoriety. Yet for all their disparities, they had one thing in common: They were all starting from scratch.

In that amorphous field of endeavor that has come to be known as military intelligence, Americans of the 1860s had no continuing national tradition upon which to build. To be sure, General George Washington had been a gifted spymaster who, during the American Revolution, had advanced from his own pocket more than $17,000 (a very large sum in those days, for which he subsequently billed Congress) to finance espionage and counterespionage activities. Especially in and around New York City, where British headquarters were located, Washington organized an intelligence network that picked up information leading to the capture of British Major John André and the resulting exposure of Benedict Arnold.

The most famous of Washington's agents was one who got caught: Nathan Hale, a young man of admirable patriotism, proved a hopeless bungler as a spy. And while Hale's courageous confrontation with the hangman would earn him martyrdom, the work of far more proficient Revolutionary spies would, by the very reason of their success in maintaining secrecy, remain almost entirely unknown for more than a century.

At any event, once the Revolutionary War ended, the members of General Washington's apparatus went their separate ways, and the United States remained without an intelligence service. The War of 1812 generated little intelligence activity on the American side. In the Mexican War, General Winfield Scott hired one Manuel Dominguez, a Mexican national and famous highwayman, to organize a number of his countrymen to scout on behalf of the Americans. The Spy Company, as this band came to be known, achieved some success in revealing the troop movements of the Mexican army, but it lasted as a group only as long as the War.

Thus as the Civil War approached, neither the Union nor the Confederacy had a formal intelligence apparatus in place — or any significant body of recorded experience to turn to for help. Both for the organizers of espionage networks and for their agents in the field, the Civil War from beginning to end was a groping process of self-education, more often marked by spectacular failures than by substantial successes.

Yet despite the amateurish methods of most and the bizarre behavior of some, many Civil War spies and other irregulars, by their burning zeal, inventive minds and cold courage, put their own stamp on the War — and though they could not change its outcome, they influenced its nature in ways that defy measurement.

Lincoln stands with other dignitaries on a well-guarded platform in front of Philadelphia's Independence Hall at a flag-raising ceremony in honor of Washington's Birthday. Later that day the President-elect, whose life had been threatened, would disappear from public view for the final stages of his journey to Washington.

During the first months of the War no individual dominated the secret struggle between raw and fumbling intelligence agents more than Allan Pinkerton, the grim little Scotsman who stood armed vigil on the darkened railroad car that bore Abraham Lincoln toward his destiny.

Pinkerton was born in Glasgow, the son of a police sergeant who was crippled by injuries sustained in workers' riots when Allan was 10 years old. After working as a barrelmaker's apprentice, Pinkerton emigrated to the United States, where he settled in Dundee, a village of Scots on the Fox River in Illinois, and set up shop as a barrelmaker. One day while on a river island cutting wood for his barrels, he chanced upon a hideout for counterfeiters. Returning to Dundee, he rounded up a group of citizens and led a raid on the island, nabbing the whole gang.

That experience gave Pinkerton a taste for law enforcement. Named a deputy sheriff in his home county in 1846, he soon sold his cooperage; then he took a job with the sheriff of Cook County, where Chicago is located. That post led to employment as the first detective on Chicago's police force. There his performance attracted the attention of several railroad presidents whose lines had recently suffered a plague of robberies. At their urging, Allan Pinkerton in 1850 resigned from the police force and set up a private detective agency, one of the nation's first. From the start, it specialized in railroad security, and by the 1860s it was flourishing.

One of Pinkerton's clients was the Philadelphia, Wilmington & Baltimore Railroad, whose tracks provided a vital link between the nation's capital and the cities of the industrial Northeast. As war approached, the

BOY WITH CONFEDERATE COCKADE IN HAT

GIRL WITH CONFEDERATE RIBBONS ON SLEEVES

A Rash of Sedition in Rebellious Marylan

A plot to assassinate President-elect Abraham Lincoln, hatched in Baltimore, was far from the only threat to the Federal government posed in volatile Maryland. The state fairly boiled with anti-Union agitation throughout the spring and summer of 1861.

The most violent outbreak occurred on Apr. 19, when Baltimore's gangs, long notorious for their lawlessness, actually attacked the 6th Massachusetts Infantry as that regiment moved through the city on its way to Washington. Other Federal troops, roughly 1,000 in number, soon occupied the city, cooling the ardor of the toughs, while still more soldiers tried to root out prosecessionist plotters elsewhere in the state. Goaded by this armed Federal presence, however, many Marylanders, including women and children, continued to flaunt their Confederate sympathies until the Union troops were withdrawn in 1862.

A Baltimore belle boldly parades past a group of Federal soldiers while wearing a dress that incorporates the Confederate Stars and Bars.

Rock-throwing Baltimoreans assault the 6th Massachusetts as the regiment makes its way between the President Street and Camden Street railroad stations.

Searching the home of a suspected Confederate sympathizer in southern Maryland, Federal soldiers confiscate hidden weapons while a sergeant reads documents that he has found.

(1.) THE ALARM.

"On Thursday night, after he had retired, Mr. LINCOLN was aroused, and informed that a stranger desired to see him on a matter of life and death. * * * A conversation elicited the fact that an organized body of men had determined that Mr. LINCOLN should never leave the City of Baltimore alive. * * * Statesmen laid the plan, Bankers indorsed it, and Adventurers were to carry it into effect."

(2.) THE COUNCIL.

"Mr. LINCOLN did not want to yield, and his friends cried with indignation. But the insisted, and he left."

railroad became woefully vulnerable in its passage through Maryland, a border state throbbing with Southern sentiment. The situation caused PW & B President Samuel H. Felton so much concern that, early in 1861, he summoned Allan Pinkerton from Chicago. Wrote Felton to the detective: "We have good reason to suspect that secessionist plotters in Maryland intend destroying the property of the road, in order to cut off the Government at Washington from the Northern States."

In Baltimore, Pinkerton observed the action. Proslavery toughs known as Blood Tubs roamed the streets, and local dandies thronged the bars of Barnum's Hotel and nearby Guy's Restaurant, purpling the atmosphere with talk of sedition. Shortly after Pinkerton's arrival, an eloquent young man began mingling with the fire-eaters, matching them boast for boast and identifying himself as one Joe Howard of Louisiana.

Pinkerton wrote later that Howard was, in fact, one of his operatives. The man's real name was Harry Davies, and he spoke in liquid accents acquired while living for several years in New Orleans. Before long, Davies ingratiated himself with one of the noisiest of the barflies, a youth of good family named Hill who was a lieutenant in the Palmetto Guards, one of several volunteer military organizations already drilling in Baltimore with the declared intention of taking arms against the United States. From his conversations with Hill the detective became convinced that an actual scheme — far more substantial and sinister than mere whiskey talk — existed to assassinate President-elect Abraham Lincoln as he passed through Baltimore on his way to be inaugurated in Washington.

According to Hill, the leader of the conspiracy was an Italian known only as Captain Ferrandini, a barber at Barnum's Hotel and captain of the Constitutional Guards, another of the treasonous local military societies. Hill further confided to Davies that the actual assassin would be selected by lot

A series of cartoons published in March 1861 lampoons Lincoln's clandestine trip through Baltimore to the capital. Anti-Lincoln newspapers gleefully — but quite incorrectly — reported that the President-elect had disguised himself for the journey in an absurdly long military cloak and an over-size Scottish tam *(opposite).*

(3.) THE SPECIAL TRAIN.
"He wore a Scotch plaid Cap and a very long Military Cloak, so that he was entirely ~~r~~ecognizable."

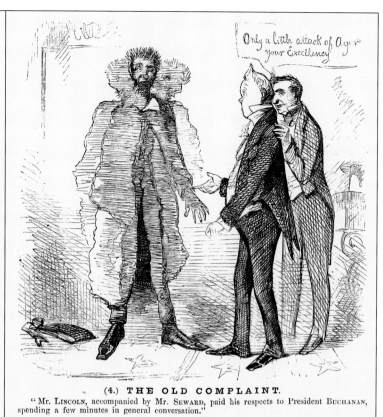

Only a little attack of Ague your Excellency!

(4.) THE OLD COMPLAINT.
"Mr. LINCOLN, accompanied by Mr. SEWARD, paid his respects to President BUCHANAN, spending a few minutes in general conversation."

from among the plotters. "Should I be chosen," said Hill, "I'll not fear to kill. Caesar was stabbed by Brutus — and Brutus was an honorable man. Lincoln need expect no mercy from me."

Worming his way still further into the conspiratorial circle, Davies was introduced by Hill to Ferrandini, who took a fancy to the detective and invited him to attend a meeting of the potential assassins. Ferrandini, overcome by violent emotion, drew from his coat a long, glittering knife and, waving it aloft, exclaimed: "This hireling Lincoln shall never, never be President!"

By this time Pinkerton had adopted the *nom de guerre* — E. J. Allen — that he was to retain so successfully throughout his wartime service. And it was as E. J. Allen, a resident of Georgia, that, through Davies, he met Ferrandini at 3 o'clock one afternoon in Guy's Restaurant. As Pinkerton wrote later, Ferrandini "cordially grasped my hand, and we all retired to a private saloon, where after ordering the necessary drinks and

cigars, the conversation became general."

In fact, Ferrandini talked specifically about the assassination conspiracy, implicating Baltimore's Police Superintendent, George P. Kane, an ardent secessionist, as someone who was sympathetic to the plot. Ferrandini then declared: "In a week from today, the North shall want another President, for Lincoln will be a corpse."

By now Pinkerton had all the details he needed. Abraham Lincoln had already left Springfield, Illinois, on what was scheduled to be a triumphal, 12-day, five-state trip that was to bring him to Washington late on the afternoon of February 23. On the last leg of the trip, the train would stop in Baltimore, where Lincoln would doubtless get off to mingle with the crowd. At that point, Kane's police would allow themselves to be distracted by a brawl staged by Blood Tubs, and during the ensuing confusion, an assassin would strike down the President-elect.

The murder would signal an uprising throughout Maryland, with insurrectionists burning railroad bridges and rolling stock, thereby isolating the capital of a leaderless nation. Meanwhile the assassin should have little difficulty in making his way from friendly Baltimore to the Chesapeake Bay, where a swift steamer would be waiting to take him to safety in the South.

About all that remained was the selection of a killer — and for that the treacherous Ferrandini had a trick up his sleeve. So deeply had Detective Harry Davies managed to penetrate into the conspiracy that he was invited to attend the secret meeting of about 30 men at which ballots would be drawn — with the one marked in red designating Lincoln's assassin. But Davies' young friend Hill told the detective that he had discovered that Ferrandini planned to place not one but eight red ballots in the box, thereby greatly boosting the chances that the President-elect would actually be assassinated.

In the event, Davies drew a white ballot — and was mildly amused to see, from the evident look of relief on his face, that Hill had done the same. Still, the fact remained that there were now eight unidentified men under oath to murder the President-elect of the United States — and it was with that chilling news that Allan Pinkerton took a train to Philadelphia, where Lincoln was due to arrive on the afternoon of February 21.

In a room at Philadelphia's Continental Hotel, Pinkerton outlined the assassination plot to its intended victim. Only a few others were present, including Pinkerton's employer, railroad President Samuel Felton, who had, independently of the detective, received word from an old Southern friend that schemes were afoot against Lincoln's life. (The informant, identified only as a Miss Dix, was described by Felton as being loyal to her native region but unable to "condone bloodshed and murder.")

Given the fantastic aspects of Pinkerton's account, and especially the role of the wild-eyed barber Ferrandini, Lincoln was naturally incredulous. "Then do I understand, sir," he asked, "that my life is chiefly threatened by this half-crazed foreigner?" Replied Pinkerton: "Mr. President, he only talks like a maniac. Ferrandini's capacity to do you harm must not be minimized. Their conspiracy is a going concern."

Abraham Lincoln was nothing if not a shrewd lawyer, and after a lengthy cross-examination of Pinkerton failed to dent the detective's story, he was at least partly convinced of its substance. Still, Lincoln postponed until the next day, when he was committed to attend Washington's Birthday ceremonies in both Philadelphia and Harrisburg, a decision on Pinkerton's plea that he change his publicly announced schedule and submit to the extraordinary measure of being taken secretly to Washington in the night.

Only a few hours after Pinkerton had offered his warning, Lincoln received corroboration from another source. A Congressional Investigating Committee, acting on advice from the U.S. Army's General in Chief Winfield Scott, had appointed John A. Kennedy, New York City's Police Superintendent, to look into the dangers of Lincoln's planned journey south. Kennedy dispatched detectives to Maryland; although the exact extent of their discoveries remains unknown, it is certain that they learned enough to report that Lincoln's life would be in peril during his passage through Baltimore.

Kennedy delivered the findings to Colonel Charles P. Stone, Inspector General of the

Fort Lafayette, a frowning pile on an island in New York harbor, was built shortly after the War of 1812 as part of New York City's defenses.

Pro-Southern Baltimoreans cheer captured Confederate troops being taken to prison in vans.

Bastilles of the North

The Federal government believed Maryland to be such a dangerous breeding ground of conspiracy that it suspended habeas corpus there and arrested without warrant 23 members of the state legislature as well as a number of other prominent citizens. Some of the notables — pictures of 12 of them are shown on the following pages — were indeed vocal Confederate sympathizers; but few were actively plotting insurrection.

Nevertheless they were imprisoned, some for more than a year, in a succession of grim old coastal fortresses, the worst being New York's Fort Lafayette. "When I think of the outrageous manner in which I have been treated, dragged from my home at midnight without a moment's warning or preparation; transported from fort to fort like a felon," wrote Lawrence Sangston in his published diary, *The Bastiles of the North*, "I do a deal of inward swearing." Sangston's fellow prisoner, Francis Key Howard, vented his anger even more bluntly, calling the Lincoln government "as vulgar and brutal a despotism as modern times have witnessed."

Inmates of Distinction

GEORGE P. KANE
Baltimore Police Superintendent

LAWRENCE SANGSTON
Maryland Legislature

BEALE RICHARDSON
Editor, Baltimore *Republican*

GEORGE WILLIAM BROWN
Mayor of Baltimore

THOMAS W. HALL
Editor, Baltimore *South*

J. H. GORDON
Maryland Legislature

JOHN B. MCMASTER
Maryland Legislature

WILLIAM WILKINS GLENN
Co-owner, Baltimore *Daily Exchange*

CHARLES HOWARD
Commissioner of Baltimore Police

T. PARKIN SCOTT
Maryland Legislature

FRANCIS KEY HOWARD
Editor, Baltimore *Daily Exchange*

SEVERN TEACKLE WALLIS
Maryland Legislature

19

Long Days in Prison

Imprisoned Marylanders complained bitterly about their lot. Quarters in Fort Lafayette were "horribly close and damp," wrote Lawrence Sangston. He noted that drinking water — taken from foul cisterns — presented a special problem: "Each glass would average a dozen tadpoles."

But prison routine was brightened considerably from time to time, thanks to sympathetic New Yorkers who sent cases of wine to the Marylanders along with food, clothing and blankets. Among the most generous donors, said Sangston, was Mrs. George Gelston who dispatched "provisions, fruits and flowers" almost daily. Such benefactors enabled the jailed men to enjoy an occasional feast, such as one described by Sangston as including "cold ducks, pickles, brandy peaches, cheese, biscuits &c." — all washed down with champagne.

District of Columbia Militia and, as such, the closest thing to a security chief that the U.S. Army then possessed. After consulting with Scott, Colonel Stone sought the help of New York's veteran Senator William H. Seward, who had already been chosen to become Lincoln's Secretary of State. And so it came to pass that around 10 o'clock on the night of February 21, Seward's son Frederick arrived in Philadelphia by train bearing letters of warning to Lincoln from his father, General Scott, and Colonel Stone, who specifically urged "a change in the traveling arrangements which would bring Mr. Lincoln through Baltimore by a night train without previous notice."

That clinched it. Although Lincoln insisted that he must keep a scheduled appearance in Harrisburg the next day, he agreed to put his life in Pinkerton's hands. And on the night of February 22, the little detective stood vigil on the rear platform of Lincoln's train, peering into the darkness for a glimpse of his agents and the more than 200 security guards hired by the railroad, who had been stationed at every bridge and road crossing between Harrisburg and Baltimore. As the train sped past, each watchman in his turn raised a lantern to signal that all was well.

Baltimore was of course the point of greatest peril, and the danger that lurked there was greatly compounded by the crude railroad facilities of the day. After Lincoln's train pulled into Baltimore's Calvert Street depot about 3:30 a.m., his car, like all other Washington-bound cars, had to be drawn separately by horses for a distance through the city streets to the Camden Station, whence another locomotive would haul them to their destination.

During this brief trek Lincoln's sleeper was at its most vulnerable, and Pinkerton was in an agony of anxiety. Yet the transfer was made without incident. "The city was in profound repose as we passed through," Pinkerton wrote later. "Darkness and silence reigned over all." At the Camden Station, however, Pinkerton was frustrated to find that the engine that would pull Lincoln's car to Washington had not yet arrived, and for more than an hour the President-elect and his party were forced to wait — while outside on the platform a drunk sang "Dixie" over and over again.

Finally the train got under way, and at 6 a.m. on February 23, as it came to a halt in the nation's capital, Abraham Lincoln unlimbered his long legs and said: "Well, boys, thank God this prayer meeting is over."

In the meantime, Ferrandini and nearly all of his fellow conspirators, having heard of Lincoln's safe passage and realizing that their game was up, had fled, presumably to the South. One who remained, however, was Police Superintendent Kane. He was later arrested in a general roundup of seditious Maryland officials.

After he returned to Chicago, Pinkerton resumed his regular vocation of catching common criminals — but not for long. In late April — less than two weeks after the fall of Fort Sumter, and even as Baltimore erupted in riots aimed at preventing Federal troops from moving through the city to Washington — Allan Pinkerton was summoned to consult with President Lincoln and several members of his Cabinet. The purpose, Pinkerton wrote, was to explore the possibility of organizing a government secret service in order to probe "the social, political and patriotic status of the numerous suspected persons in and around the city."

During these discussions, however, it became increasingly evident to Pinkerton that because of "the novel and perplexing" conditions of a nation newly embroiled in civil war, "anything approaching a systematized organization or operation would be for a time impossible."

Pinkerton thereupon departed the capital, but he had not progressed far before receiving a message from an old friend — Major General George B. McClellan. One of West Point's more promising graduates, McClellan had seemed a rising star in the old Army until, in 1857, he resigned to become chief engineer of the Illinois Central Railroad. In that capacity and, later, as president of the Ohio & Mississippi Railroad, McClellan had employed Pinkerton for security purposes and had thought highly of both the man and his work. Now, as a major general of Ohio

Volunteers, he perceived a need for the detective — who happily answered McClellan's invitation to become a member of the general's staff.

On July 27, 1861, less than a week after the shocking Union defeat at Bull Run, General McClellan, fresh from a successful campaign in the mountains of western Virginia, arrived in Washington to assume command of the Army of the Potomac. With him was Allan Pinkerton, or Major E. J. Allen, who had been ordered to form what, years later, he would insist on calling the "United States Secret Service."

In fact, it was never officially designated as such. During the Civil War, "secret service" was a generic term used to describe any organization that gathered information by covert means. Moreover, Pinkerton's agency was in no sense a national network. It was organized to operate under a rather peculiar arrange-

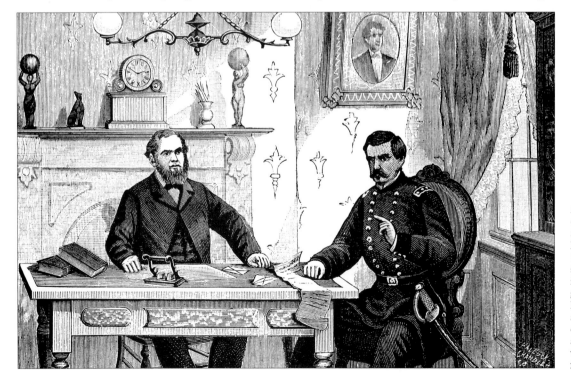

At General George McClellan's Cincinnati headquarters, McClellan and Allan Pinkerton plan Pinkerton's spying trip into the South in 1861. It proved an adventurous mission. Spotted as a Union agent while in Memphis, the detective escaped by galloping out of town on a swift horse. Then in Jackson, Mississippi, a barber who had once worked in Chicago greeted Pinkerton effusively as an old customer. His identity revealed, Pinkerton again departed at full speed on horseback.

ment: When McClellan took to the field (which he was remarkably slow about doing), Pinkerton would go along as a staff member in charge of gathering information about the enemy. While in Washington, however, Pinkerton would receive his orders from the civilian authorities of the War Department, and his job would be to "test all suspected persons" in a city where secessionist sentiment ran high and hot among a large minority of the population.

"I was soon hard at work in my efforts to 'regulate' the District of Columbia," Pinkerton later recalled. Indeed, hardly had he settled into his headquarters than Assistant Secretary of War Thomas A. Scott instructed him to "watch a lady whose movements had excited suspicion."

The woman was Rose O'Neal Greenhow, an attractive widow with extensive connections on both sides of the conflict. Born in Maryland to a family of modest means, the dark, lissome Rose had come to Washington as a girl, living with an aunt who kept a boardinghouse in the Old Capitol building. Used as temporary quarters for Congress after British soldiers burned Washington's public buildings during the War of 1812, the dingy brick structure had since fallen into disrepair. But, because of its convenient location, it was tenanted by several members of Congress — chief among them the fierce old "Father of Secession," South Carolina's John C. Calhoun. The young Rose O'Neal adored Calhoun, and from him she inherited the political sentiments to which she would devote herself until the day of her death.

At the age of 26, Rose married a man 17 years her senior. Dr. Robert Greenhow was a physician who had turned to more academic pursuits and, while serving as a translator for the State Department, was writing an authoritative history of Tripoli. Though he belonged to a distinguished Virginia family and was well placed in Washington society, Greenhow was not wealthy; when he died in 1854 he left his widow and four daughters little more than a small brick house on 16th Street, across from St. John's Church.

Forced to live by her wits, Mrs. Greenhow used her political friendships to obtain jobs and promotions for those who were willing to contribute to her upkeep. Her career as a hostess and informal power broker reached its zenith during the Administration of the bachelor President James Buchanan, who raised capital eyebrows by the frequency of his visits to her home, which was only a brief carriage ride from the White House.

But Buchanan was by no means the only powerful citizen to pay his respects. Before leaving Washington to take up more pressing tasks, Mississippi's Senator Jefferson Davis had sometimes attended Rose Greenhow's salons. So did Oregon's Senator Joseph Lane, who wrote her a note one day complaining that she was "always surrounded by admirers" — and vowing to return at 9 p.m., when conditions would presumably be less crowded. Still another regular guest was New York Republican Seward, a stern man during business hours but — as Rose snidely wrote after the two had become enemies — one likely to become "properly attuned" after supper and "under the influence of the generous gifts the gods provide."

The most devoted admirer of all was the pudgy, scowling, abolitionist Senator from Massachusetts, Henry Wilson. Found in Mrs. Greenhow's possession a few months after the outbreak of war were several passionate love letters, signed *H* and written on

Senate stationery in a hand that strongly resembled Wilson's. Although positive proof of Wilson's authorship has never been found, there is no doubt whatever that during a critical period in America, the Chairman of the Senate Military Affairs Committee — a man privy to many of the nation's most vital secrets — was sharing more than tea and crumpets with a Confederate spy.

For Rose Greenhow was indeed a spy — and she had been recruited at least partly because of her relationship with Henry Wilson.

The man who enlisted Rose Greenhow as a spy was Captain Thomas Jordan, an assistant quartermaster on the War Department staff. Of the scores of U.S. Army officers who gave up their commissions and went to the South, Jordan was one of the very last to leave Washington, departing not until May 21 — more than five weeks after the fall of Fort Sumter. During that interim Jordan had been very busy indeed — completing his arrangements for what was almost certainly the infant Confederacy's first spy ring, with none other than Rose Greenhow as its operating head.

A graduate of West Point, where he had roomed with a cadet named William Tecumseh Sherman, the Virginia-born Jordan, having long since made up his mind to join the Confederacy, could foresee an urgent need for military intelligence about such matters as Federal supply needs, troop strength, troop movements and plans.

As it happened, Jordan was also something of a man about town. As he later confided to a friend, while circulating in Washington's active salon circuit he had learned of an "intimacy" existing between Rose O'Neal Greenhow and Senator Henry Wilson. After

discovering that relationship, it was evidently no difficult feat for the handsome, persuasive Jordan to establish, as he put it, "the same kind of intimacy" with Rose, whereupon he "induced her to get from Wilson all the information she could."

By the time of Jordan's departure, however, the espionage effort had greatly expanded. Among other things, Jordan, who was already slated to become adjutant general of the Confederate forces gathering at the nearby railroad junction of Manassas, gave Rose a cipher of his own invention by which she could communicate with him through a secret courier system.

Beyond that, Captain Jordan and Mrs. Greenhow worked together to select and recruit other members for the spy ring. Although its full roster will probably never be known, the ring certainly came to include Colonel Michael Thompson, a South Carolinian living in Washington who adopted, after his initials, the code name of Colonel Empty; William T. Smithson, a local banker; Dr. Aaron Van Camp, Rose's dentist; William Walker and F. Rennehan, both government clerks; and, acting as couriers, a housewife named Bettie Hassler, a wan spinster, Lily Mackall, who was entrapped by her blind devotion to Rose Greenhow, and young Betty Duvall, whose raven beauty would long linger in the memory of at least one Confederate general.

Thus, when the time came for Rose O'Neal Greenhow to do her part for the Confederacy, she was more than ready. "To this end," she wrote later, "I employed every capacity with which God had endowed me."

And God had been generous. At the age of 44, Rose possessed a full figure, dark, slumberous eyes, and a magnetic personality.

Armed guards, provided with a sentry box for inclement weather, patrol the Chain Bridge across the Potomac River to prevent Confederate agents from carrying information from Washington into Virginia. The span was originally a suspension bridge supported by chains — thus its name — but by 1861 it had become a structure of wooden trusses.

Colonel Erasmus D. Keyes, a Union officer, later described Mrs. Greenhow as "the most persuasive woman that was ever known in Washington," and recalled how often he had been "lured to the brink of the precipice." (It was a good thing for the Union that Keyes resisted temptation: As military secretary to General in Chief Winfield Scott he had access to vital information.) An even more compelling testament to Rose's charms came from her nemesis, Allan Pinkerton, who in an official report paid grudging tribute to her "almost irresistible seductive powers."

In the spring the Greenhow ring swung into full operation. General Pierre Gustave Toutant Beauregard, commanding the Confederates at Manassas, later boasted: "Happily, through the foresight of Colonel Thomas Jordan, arrangements were made which enabled me to receive regularly, from private persons at the Federal capital, most accurate information. I was almost as well advised of the strength of the hostile army in my front as its commander."

By early summer it was clear that the War's first major conflict would soon take place near Manassas, and the scene in Washington grew frantic as the Union Army prepared to do battle. As Mrs. Greenhow recalled, "Officers and orderlies on horse were

25

seen flying from place to place; the tramp of armed men was heard on every side — martial music filled the air."

Given the hubbub, a spy ring was hardly necessary to tell Beauregard that Union General Irvin McDowell would soon be heading his way. But the Confederate commander faced a delicate problem in timing, and he urgently needed specific information — the exact date of the Federal march.

Beauregard had been pleading with Confederate authorities in Richmond to be reinforced immediately by the 11,000 troops under General Joseph E. Johnston, now in the Shenandoah Valley. Beauregard's requests were rejected on grounds that Johnston's force was needed to prevent a Union army under General Robert Patterson from overrunning the valley. It was understood, however, that Johnston's brigades would be rushed to Manassas — when and if Beauregard could present definite evidence that he was about to be attacked.

That evidence was at least partly provided by Rose Greenhow and her comrades in espionage. On the morning of July 10, Betty Duvall, the daughter of respectable Marylanders who had moved to Washington, dressed up as a country lass, took the reins of a farm cart and around noon crossed the Chain Bridge into Virginia. After spending the night with the family of a Confederate naval officer, Betty donned a stylish riding costume and continued toward Fairfax Court House, where she was stopped by Confederate pickets and taken to General Milledge L. Bonham, one of Beauregard's brigadiers. To Bonham, Miss Duvall was "a beautiful young lady, a brunette with sparkling black eyes, perfect features and the glow of patriotic devotion burning in her face."

Before the general's admiring eyes, Betty Duvall "took out her tucking comb and let fall the longest and most beautiful roll of hair that I have ever seen." Calmly, she "took then from the back of her head, where it had been safely tied, a small package, not larger than a silver dollar, sewed up in silk."

In the packet was a note that, deciphered, said: "McDowell has certainly been ordered to advance on the sixteenth. R.O.G."

Turned over to General Beauregard, the message was then rushed by courier to Jefferson Davis in Richmond. President Davis, however, proved skeptical. He may well have been aware that one attack by McDowell on Manassas had already been scheduled and canceled, and he may have guessed that another postponement would occur. At any rate, he refused again to issue Johnston his marching orders.

Now the date specified by Rose Greenhow was drawing dangerously close — and Beauregard was desperate for up-to-the-minute information. On Beauregard's behalf, Thomas Jordan sent a spy to Mrs. Greenhow: Early on July 16, George Donellan, who had been a surveyor in the U.S. Interior Department before going South, knocked on her door and, after she had been awakened by a maid, handed her a cipher message from Jordan that said "Trust bearer."

Mrs. Greenhow confirmed her first message: The Union's General McDowell would "positively" start that very day "to advance from Arlington Heights and Alexandria on to Manassas via Fairfax Court House and Centreville." By 8 o'clock that night, Donellan was back at Beauregard's headquarters with the information.

The message was relayed to Richmond. And as McDowell advanced, orders went out to General Johnston to leave the Shenandoah Valley and join Beauregard on the banks of Bull Run. Even so, it was a narrow thing — on the morning of July 21, when McDowell's lumbering army finally launched its attack across Bull Run, Johnston's troops were still arriving on the battlefield near Manassas. Their participation would save the day for the South; within 48 hours a message from Thomas Jordan would arrive at the narrow brick house on Washington's 16th Street.

"Our President and our General direct me to thank you," Jordan had written. "We rely on your further information. The Confederacy owes you a debt."

For her success Rose Greenhow would pay a heavy price. Rose had never troubled to conceal her passionate sympathies for the Southern cause, and the War Department soon became suspicious of her clandestine activities. As a result, Allan Pinkerton was assigned to her case.

His first effort to get evidence against Mrs. Greenhow was, as it turned out, pure slapstick. Shortly after receiving the assignment, Pinkerton and two of his men took station outside the Greenhow house. The day had been dark and brooding, and now, as Pinkerton would recall, a "storm burst upon us in all its fury. Umbrellas were a useless commodity, and, unprotected, we were compelled to breast the elements, which were now warring with terrible violence."

Noting that a light shone through a window above his head, Pinkerton removed his boots, clambered on the shoulders of his assistants and looked in — but, to his great disappointment, found the room empty.

Just then footsteps were heard approaching the house. Jumping down from his perch, Pinkerton hid with his aides beneath the front stoop of Rose's house. Someone climbed the steps above their heads, rang the doorbell and was soon admitted.

Back at the window, Pinkerton this time was rewarded by the sight of an Army captain whom he instantly recognized as being in charge of one of the offices of the provost marshal. Although the man appeared nervous at first, Pinkerton recalled, his "face lighted up with pleasure" when Mrs. Greenhow entered the room. "Presently," Pinkerton's account continued, "he took from an inner pocket of his coat a map which, as he held it up before the light, I imagined that I could identify as a plan of the fortifications in and around Washington. My blood boiled with indignation."

Even as the pair was studying the map, the sound of a passerby sent the detectives scrambling beneath the stoop, and by the time Pinkerton returned to the window, "the delectable couple had disappeared." Pinkerton kept a vigil, peering occasionally into the room. An hour passed before the two reappeared and the captain prepared to leave. Back under the stoop went the detectives, while overhead they heard "a whispered good-night, and something that sounded very much like a kiss."

As the captain moved into the tempest, Pinkerton followed, leaving behind his assistants as well as his boots. He was confident, he said later, that he "would not be detected as, in my drenched stockings, I crept along as stealthily as a cat."

Yet something went awry. At the corner of 15th Street and Pennsylvania Avenue, his quarry suddenly ducked into a building. When Pinkerton followed, he was confronted by four soldiers with fixed bayonets. Only

The Confederate agent Rose Greenhow hugs her daughter, "Little Rose," while both were confined in the Old Capitol building in Washington. To spite her captors, Mrs. Greenhow allowed Little Rose to approach starvation rather than let her eat prison fare.

then did he realize that the captain, aware that he was being tailed, had gone into his own barracks and ordered his soldiers to arrest the man following him.

Clapped behind bars, Pinkerton languished for hours before finally bribing a guard to send word of his plight to the War Department. After Pinkerton's release, the errant captain was arrested.

As for Rose Greenhow, Pinkerton was not yet ready to pounce. She still had powerful friends in government, and Pinkerton was under orders to move cautiously. Her house was therefore kept under constant surveil-

lance, and the woman herself was watched wherever she went on her daily promenades. (Mrs. Greenhow knew that she was being followed and, far from being fazed, seemed to enjoy all the attention she was getting.) Bit by bit and piece by piece the evidence accumulated — until, on August 23, Pinkerton made his move.

On that day, as Mrs. Greenhow was returning to her home from a walk, she was confronted by Pinkerton, who was wearing a uniform with a major's insignia. Pinkerton asked: "You're Mrs. Greenhow?"

"Yes," said Rose. And then she asked: "Who are you, and what do you want here?"

Said Pinkerton: "I've come to arrest you."

At that point Mrs. Greenhow asked to see a warrant. In fact, Pinkerton had neglected to obtain legal papers — but this was war, and warrant or not, Allan Pinkerton would do his duty as he saw it. Escorting Mrs. Greenhow into her house, Pinkerton ordered a top-to-bottom search that uncovered a wealth of incriminating evidence including the love letters — signed *H* — that were thought to come from Henry Wilson, a letter in cipher from Mrs. Greenhow to Jordan, a note from Donellan and wads of shredded correspondence. In hopes that other members of the ring might visit Rose during the day, Pinkerton instructed his men to stay inside the house and lay low. An occurrence soon conspired against him: Mrs. Greenhow's eight-year-old daughter, also named Rose, managed to get out and climb a tree, from which she trilled to everyone who came within earshot "Mama's been arrested! Mama's been arrested!" Little Rose was quickly pulled out of the tree and put back indoors with her mother. In spite of her display, several Confederate sympathizers called at the house later that day and were immediately arrested as suspected spies.

Not until nearly 4 o'clock the next morning was Rose Greenhow finally allowed to retire after what she demurely described as a "most trying day." There would be more days as bad or worse. Instead of carting Mrs. Greenhow off to jail, Union authorities kept her at home under round-the-clock surveillance by male guards — a fact that, when it became known, aroused indignation throughout the South. "For eight days," wrote the South Carolina diarist Mary Boykin Chesnut, "she was kept in full sight of men, her rooms wide open, and sleepless sentinels watching by day and by night.

In this melodramatic etching, Federal agent John Scobell coolly shoots down a pair of Confederate cavalrymen who were pursuing him and another Union spy, Hattie Lawton, as they fled the Richmond area. The two agents then found safety behind Union lines. Scobell was one of several black men who proved to be daring and canny agents in Allan Pinkerton's secret service.

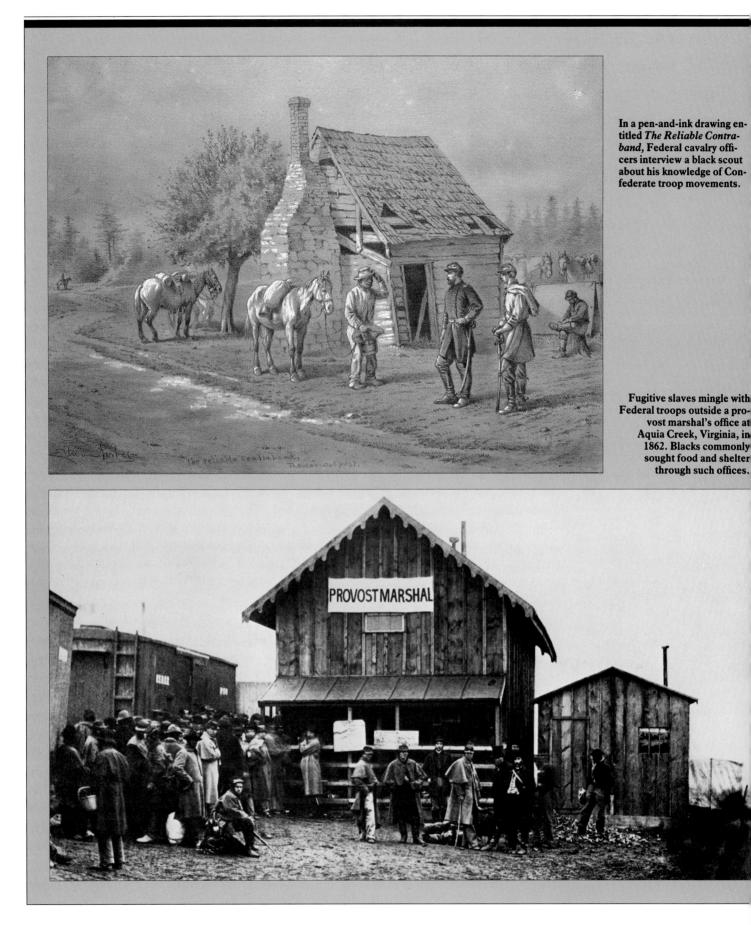

In a pen-and-ink drawing entitled *The Reliable Contraband,* Federal cavalry officers interview a black scout about his knowledge of Confederate troop movements.

Fugitive slaves mingle with Federal troops outside a provost marshal's office at Aquia Creek, Virginia, in 1862. Blacks commonly sought food and shelter through such offices.

A Harvest of Intelligence from Runaway Slaves

The Federal armies in the field could count on gleaning much valuable intelligence from a huge reservoir of willing informers — fugitive slaves who, having fled to freedom behind Union lines, gladly described what they had observed of the Confederates' fortifications, troop dispositions and supply operations. Although a majority of the blacks decided to continue on their way to refugee camps provided for them, a few did agree to remain near the fighting fronts and actively serve with Federal scouting parties (left).

The task of gathering and organizing the information offered by the "contrabands," as the runaways were called, fell to the provost marshal, who combined such intelligence work with military police duties. The most celebrated officer to hold that post was Marsena R. Patrick, who became Provost Marshal General of the Army of the Potomac in September of 1862. As the opposing forces maneuvered in Virginia, Patrick was usually well versed in the Confederate order of battle. One group of Confederate prisoners, Patrick wrote, "were very much disgusted when they found that I knew their organization and called out their regiments as readily as I would our own."

Described by a biographer as possessing "the air of an Old Testament prophet" and a fierce temper to match his appearance, the irascible General Marsena Patrick stands at his headquarters tent near Brandy Station, Virginia, in 1864.

Beautiful as she is, even at her time of life, few women like all the mysteries of their toilette laid bare to the public eye."

At the end of August 1861 it was decided to turn Mrs. Greenhow's home into a detention center not only for its owner but for several other women suspected of spying for the Confederacy. Confinement in "Fort Greenhow," as it came to be known, was made unpleasant by the fact that the women, despite the commonality of their cause, did not get along. Mrs. Greenhow, for example, refused to talk with another inmate, saying that she was "generally of the lowest class," while still another "raved from early morn till late at night, in language more vehement than delicate."

For five months, while tourists thronged outside in hope of glimpsing a spy, the women remained in Fort Greenhow, and Rose mourned that, "My castle has become my prison." In January 1862 the occupants were transferred to the Old Capitol — where the young Rose O'Neal had lived with her aunt and succumbed to the secessionist enchantments of John C. Calhoun — now converted from a boardinghouse into a jail.

And there she stayed until June 2, 1862, when she was finally released and sent South. That summer Rose was dispatched by the Confederacy to England and France on a secret mission whose purpose remains unknown, and she remained abroad for more than two years, meanwhile writing her memoirs. On September 30, 1864, she was returning to the United States aboard the blockade runner *Condor* when it ran ashore off the coast of North Carolina.

Rose O'Neal Greenhow drowned in the wreck. Then and thereafter, some would dispute the substantive value of her service to

the Confederacy. But Rose had known better. After all, she had the word of the man who greeted her in Richmond after her release from incarceration. "But for you," Jefferson Davis had said, "there would have been no Bull Run."

In his efforts to secure the safety of the President and defend the Union against espionage, Allan Pinkerton had been successful. Yet this was hardly surprising, since these were the sorts of endeavor to which he could apply his vast experience as a private investigator. But in the less familiar field of combat intelligence — the analysis of military information — Pinkerton would forge a legacy of incompetence.

Pinkerton's failure was not for lack of energy and organization; by any measure, the amount of information he collected was prodigious. "My system of obtaining knowledge," Pinkerton wrote long after the War, "was so thorough and complete, my sources of information were so varied, that there could be no serious mistake in the estimates which I then made and reported to General McClellan." In gathering information, Pinkerton relied heavily on spies of his own. "My shrewd and daring operatives," he recalled, "men and women, trained for the work, moved in and out among the Rebel troops at all times and places."

In Pinkerton's stable of agents were a number of colorful characters who provided useful information. Among them were John Scobell, a former slave in Mississippi who could sing Scottish ballads (taught him by a former master) with all the verve, said Pinkerton, of "the feathered songsters that warbled in the tropical groves of his own sunny home"; "Stuttering Dave" Graham, who

posed as an itinerant peddler during his trips into Virginia and, beyond his disarming stammer, could work his way out of tight spots by faking a most convincing — and very distractive — epileptic fit; and, not least, the ill-fated Timothy Webster (*pages 34-43*), a devoted Pinkerton man who traveled the South on a pass granted him by the Confederacy's Secretary of War.

As compiled from information provided by his agents and other sources, Pinkerton's reports to General McClellan were models of their kind, not only identifying enemy units but offering an extraordinary amount of minutiae about morale, supplies and equipment — right down to a description of the buttons on Confederate uniforms. Such information might have been enormously useful, but it was in the most important category of all — estimates of the enemy's strength — that Pinkerton veered into fantasy.

Exactly what went wrong may never be known. Most of Pinkerton's records, which presumably described his techniques, were destroyed by the great fire that swept Chicago in 1871. It is certain, however, that Pinkerton devised some sort of formula by

which he translated the numbers given him by his agents into estimates of enemy strength. And through inexperience he routinely provided for wide margins of error in his calculations, ostensibly to account for supposed new arrivals of recent recruits to Confederate units.

The results were often ludicrous. In October 1861, for example, McClellan used Pinkerton's intelligence report to declare that Confederate General Joseph Johnston had massed in the vicinity of Manassas a force "not less than 150,000 strong, well drilled and equipped, ably commanded, and strongly intrenched." In fact, Johnston had no more than 50,000 troops.

After transporting more than 120,000 men to Virginia's Peninsula in early April 1862, McClellan bogged down in front of Yorktown for more than a month, largely because Pinkerton advised him that he was confronted by as many as 120,000 hostile troops. That estimate, Pinkerton later said, was partly based on information from "persons well connected with the Confederate commissary department" who told Union spies

that 119,000 rations were being issued daily. In reality, McClellan faced fewer than 17,000 Confederates under Brigadier General John Bankhead Magruder.

As McClellan's massive army slowly shouldered its way up the Peninsula, the Confederates received reinforcements, but in Pinkerton's imagination the enemy numbers grew disproportionately. By June 26, Pinkerton's organization, in a masterpiece of combat intelligence, had correctly identified all major Confederate units — including 208 infantry regiments, nine cavalry regiments and 39 artillery battalions. Yet in calculating General Robert E. Lee's numerical strength, Pinkerton came up with an astronomical 180,000 — when in fact the Confederates numbered 50,000. The cautious McClellan, always ready to believe the worst, virtually gave up hope for his army, declaring himself ready and willing "at least to die with it and share its fate."

In late summer of 1862, Lee's invasion of Maryland caught Pinkerton without his spies in place, and for better or for worse, he contributed little to the ensuing campaign. After the Battle of Antietam, McClellan was removed from command of the Army of the Potomac, and Allan Pinkerton followed his beloved chief back into civilian life.

In 1864 some of Pinkerton's Confederate troop estimates were made public, arousing both indignation and merriment. The essayist James Russell Lowell jeered that Pinkerton's miscalculations surpassed anything "since Don Quixote's enumeration of the armies of the Emperor Alifanfaron and King Pentapolin of the Naked Arm." It was a sorry conclusion for Pinkerton, who in other fields had performed well for his country.

TIMOTHY WEBSTER

An Agent Extraordinary

The most effective Union secret agent of the early war years was a daring former detective named Timothy Webster. An employee of Allen Pinkerton's before the War, Webster followed his chief into the secret service when the conflict began.

Pinkerton gave his favorite spy a series of risky missions: infiltrating pro-Southern cabals in Baltimore and traveling deep into the Confederacy to observe troop movements and other military activity. Some notable exploits of Webster's career are shown on these pages in pictures and accounts drawn from Pinkerton's postwar memoirs.

*T*imothy Webster's first assignment was to spy on Confederate army units forming in Kentucky and Tennessee. He gathered much vital information, largely by convincing Confederate officers in Memphis that he was a fire-breathing secessionist. "He practically mesmerized you into thinking he was whatever he decided to be," noted a colleague. Webster's masquerade so convinced the officers (incorrectly portrayed above in Federal uniforms) that, after several infusions of bourbon, they insisted on buying him a "secession chapeau" — a Confederate officer's hat.

Throughout his travels in the west, Webster was tailed by a tenacious counterspy suspicious of Northerners. This agent was about to arrest Webster in Humboldt, Tennessee, when the detective hid behind baggage at the railroad depot then leaped unseen onto a train that took him north toward Ohio and safety.

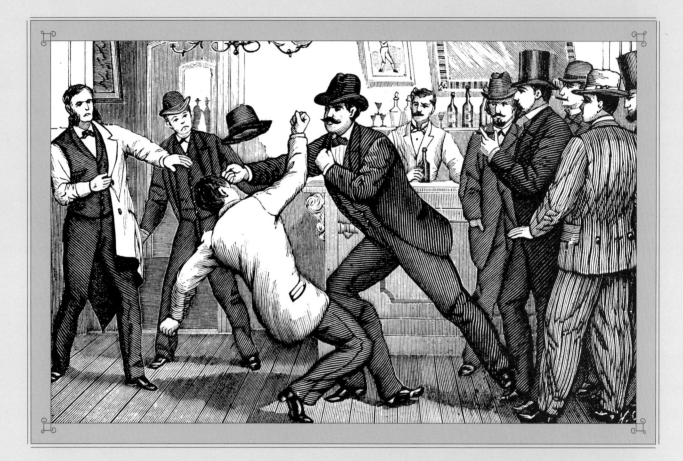

Timothy Webster's next assignment was to keep watch on nests of armed and potentially violent Confederate sympathizers in Baltimore. He very quickly gained the confidence of the leading plotters, again by posing as a diehard secessionist.

A dangerous crisis arose when a man by the name of Bill Zigler strode into a Baltimore saloon and denounced Webster to the assembled pro-Confederates. Zigler declared that *he had seen Webster entering Allan Pinkerton's offices in Washington — Webster was nothing but a Yankee spy. Webster immediately realized, Pinkerton later wrote, that Zigler's "insinuation must be denied and overcome. With an assumption of uncontrollable rage he cried out 'You are a liar and a scoundrel.' " Webster then struck Zigler (above) "with a force that would have felled an ox," knocking him under a table.*

Webster's display of righteous anger at Zigler further convinced the Baltimore secessionist plotters of his reliability. He was soon invited to join a clandestine society called the Knights of Liberty, which was said to have 6,000 weapons and was busily scheming an armed march on Washington.

Webster informed Pinkerton, who arranged a raid on one of the Knights of Liberty's midnight conclaves. A squad of Federal infantry-

men battered through the locked meeting-room door (above). "Horrified consternation was depicted on every blanched face," Pinkerton related. "The arch traitors and prime movers in the secret enterprise were taken to Fort McHenry" and imprisoned. Timothy Webster was allowed to get away after the raid, but — so great was his reputation as a secessionist — his escape aroused little suspicion among his Baltimore friends.

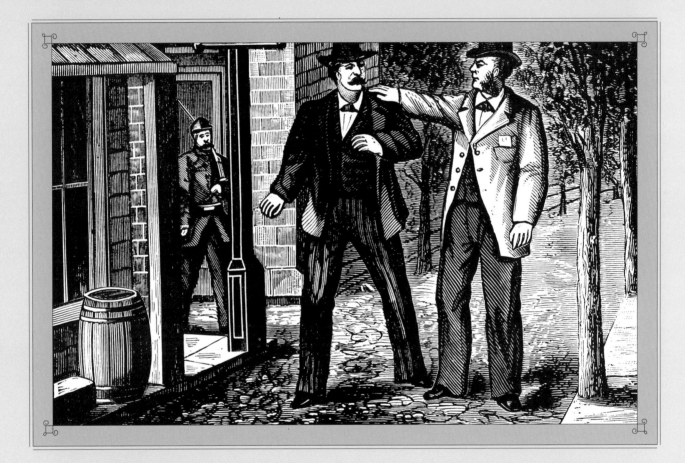

*A*nother threat to Webster's spying career soon appeared — in the form of a Federal agent. Walking down a Baltimore street one evening in late 1861, Webster sensed that he was being shadowed by a menacing-looking stranger. The next day the same man was on his heels. Then Webster felt a heavy hand on his shoulder (above) and heard the words, "You are my prisoner."

Webster was hustled into a nearby Federal guardhouse with armed sentries at the door. His captor, he realized, was a new and eager member of Pinkerton's force who, for security reasons, had not been informed of Webster's operations — and really believed Webster was a Confederate secret agent. Imprisoned for hours, Webster at length got word of his plight to Pinkerton and an order came for his release. But freedom only created a different problem for Webster.

Webster found himself in a precarious situation. He knew that word of his arrest would have spread throughout Baltimore. He could not simply walk out of a Federal guardhouse as if nothing had happened without seriously jeopardizing his reputation as one of the city's most passionate and vocal Yankee haters.

A solution was found. While a crowd of onlookers gathered that evening, Webster was marched under guard from the jail and bundled into a police van. The officer in charge then loudly ordered the driver to head for Fort McHenry, the prison on a spit of land in Baltimore harbor. But he whispered to Webster to make a run for it whenever he was ready. On the way to the fort, Webster leaped from the speeding van (above) and vanished into the night. This second dramatic escape only enhanced Webster's standing among Baltimore's Confederate sympathizers.

*H*aving helped to frustrate the secessionists in Baltimore, Timothy Webster undertook several risky missions to the Confederate capital of Richmond. He played his role so expertly that he received a government passport allowing him to travel anywhere in the South.

His third trip to Richmond proved unusually difficult. Webster followed his customary, roundabout route via southern Maryland, crossing the lower Potomac by boat to Virginia. This time he was joined by two young wives, heading south to join Confederate officer husbands, and their three children. The night was stormy, and their small vessel struck a sandbar 100 yards from the Virginia shore. Without hesitation, Webster jumped into the water and struggled to shore with two of the children (above). Then he waded out again and saved the two women and the remaining child. His heroism was soon to pay a dividend.

*W*ebster and the shivering little party made their way to a nearby farmhouse and were taken in. His struggles in the frigid Potomac were to afflict him with painful rheumatism, but that night he was rewarded. As he lay down to sleep before the fire (above), he spied on the floor an oilcloth-wrapped packet that had fallen from the garments of one of the women he had saved. It was addressed to *Judah P. Benjamin, Confederate Secretary of War.*

When he opened the packet, Webster found that it contained, as Pinkerton related, "complete maps of the country surrounding Washington, with a correct statement of the number and location of Federal troops" — information that could only have been provided by a traitor in the Federal government. Acting on Webster's information, Pinkerton soon arrested a Confederate spy in the U.S. Provost Marshal's office.

The recurring rheumatism that Webster contracted in the Potomac and the ineptitude of two fellow spies caused Webster's downfall.

Prostrated by the disease on his fourth trip to Richmond, Webster could neither return to Washington nor send secret messages to report his condition. Pinkerton, worried about his best agent, sent two less-experienced operatives, John Scully and Pryce Lewis, to Richmond to see what had happened.

Both Scully and Lewis were soon spotted as suspicious characters by Confederate authorities and arrested. It did not help matters when Lewis joined in an escape of prisoners from Henrico Jail — thereby seeming to confirm his guilt. After days of wandering in the Chickahominy swamps northeast of Richmond, he and several other escapees were recaptured (above) by Confederate pickets, who found them roasting corn over a campfire.

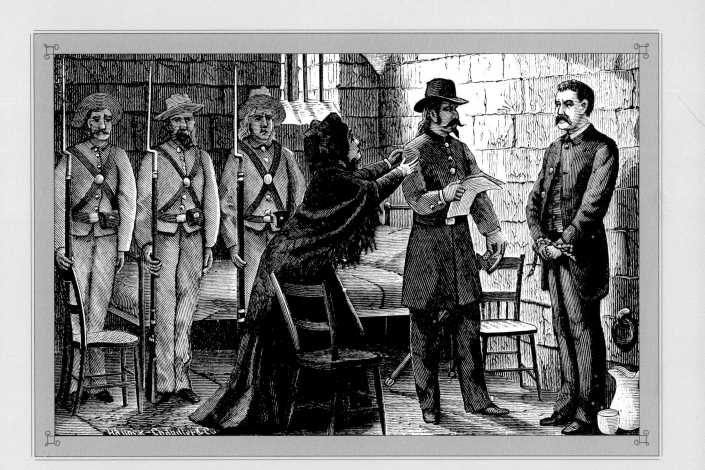

Worse, Scully and Lewis on arrival in Richmond had imprudently gone to see Webster in the hotel where he was confined to bed by his rheumatism. Their visit had thrown suspicion on Webster — a suspicion confirmed when Scully, convicted and condemned to be hanged, saved his own skin by confessing that Webster was a far more important spy than he.

Timothy Webster was swiftly arrested and tried — and condemned to death. His only sup-

port in prison came from Hattie Lawton, also a Federal spy, who was later jailed but not executed. The woman pleaded with the Confederate authorities (above) to allow Webster to be shot, as he wished, rather than make him suffer a felon's death by hanging. Her pleas were in vain; Webster was hanged on April 29, 1862. He was, wrote Pinkerton, a "faithful, brave, true-hearted man" for whom "fear was an element entirely unknown."

The Undercover Confederates

"Was it not possible that as a spy I might discover that which would soon give the Southern cause the upper hand in its struggle for Secession?"

THOMAS NELSON CONRAD, CONFEDERATE AGENT

"I am managing a good deal of the secret service & find that to do it well, I have to be utterly unscrupulous myself in words & deeds & can only hope that the end will justify the means."

Writing to his father in the winter of 1861, a Confederate captain named E. Porter Alexander thus described his role in espionage on behalf of the Confederacy. One of the first of his breed in the South during the War, young Alexander came to play a role in the clandestine arts through a process that was typical — a combination of happenstance and personal enterprise.

The chain of events that led Alexander to espionage began before the War, in October 1859, when he was a 23-year-old U.S. Army lieutenant and an assistant instructor at West Point. There, by chance, he met an Army surgeon named Albert J. Myer, who was then engaged in a nonmedical pursuit. While assigned to duty on the Western plains, Myer had become fascinated by the way Comanche warriors motioned with their lances to send messages over long distances. Using flags affixed to long staffs, Myer developed his own signal system and offered it to the War Department for adoption.

When Alexander met him, Myer was back in the East to demonstrate his new system to U.S. Army brass. Struck by Alexander's inquiring, innovative mind, Myer arranged that the West Pointer be assigned as an assistant in the signaling trials.

With Myer signaling from Alexandria, Virginia, and Alexander reading the messages through a telescope across the Potomac in Washington, a distance of six miles, the War Department test was highly successful. But before the system received final approval in February 1860, Alexander was reassigned to duty in the Far West. Then, in February 1861, his native Georgia seceded from the Union. The War began, and Alexander and Myer landed on opposite sides.

While Myer remained loyal to the Union, Alexander accepted a captain's commission in the Confederate Army. All too soon to suit Alexander's tastes, Confederate authorities recalled his experience with Myer and relegated him to the decidedly dull job of setting up a small factory to manufacture such signal apparatus as poles, flags and torches (for nighttime use). Hardly had he gone to work, however, than he was rescued by the exigencies of war and sent to Manassas as General P.G.T. Beauregard's signal officer.

In the summer of 1861, General Irvin McDowell was gathering his Union army for its advance on Bull Run. By that time Alexander had constructed four signal towers and had somehow managed to train a contingent of privates, even though the trainees were "so stupid that I have to knock them down & jump on them & stamp & pound them before I can get an idea into their heads." On the morning of July 21 Alexander was atop one of the towers, peering through a spyglass. As he scanned beyond the Confederate left, he recalled, his eye "was caught by a glitter. I

In the hollow head and body of this doll, named Nina by its young owner, desperately needed morphine and quinine from the North were smuggled into the Confederacy. With a capacity of several ounces, this and similar dolls passed comparatively easily through Federal lines in the hands of women and children. The ring, worn by a South Carolina woman, had a secret recess for coded messages written on onionskin paper.

recognized it at once as the reflection of the morning sun from a brass field-piece. Closer scrutiny soon revealed the glittering of bayonets and musket barrels."

Instantly realizing that a Federal force was moving to outflank Beauregard's army, Alexander used his signal flags to send a message directly to Colonel Nathan Evans, commanding the brigade farthest left on the Confederate line. "Look out for your left," it said, "you are turned."

Thanks to Alexander's warning, Confederate troops rushed to intercept the flanking Federals, delayed the enemy until reinforcements arrived and converted what could have been a Confederate castastrophe into a Union rout. Ironically, Alexander's former colleague, Albert Myer, Signal Officer of the U.S. Army since 1860, had failed to get his system satisfactorily organized in time for the battle at Bull Run, and Union communications were woefully inadequate there.

On the day after the Battle of Bull Run, Alexander was named Beauregard's chief of ordnance and artillery. At the same time, however, he retained his duties as the general's signal officer, and in that role Porter Alexander became involved in espionage.

As a signal officer, Alexander's primary responsibility was communications. Yet he soon discovered that communications and espionage are closely related. While the Confederate army lingered near Manassas, Alexander noticed that a mere five miles from the

Potomac River the army's picket lines ran along Mason's Hill, "from which many houses in Washington were plainly visible.

"This suggested," Alexander recalled, "opening a line of secret signals from a window in one of these houses to an observation room on the top of a residence on Mason's Hill."

To put his scheme into effect, Alexander enlisted the services of E. Pliny Bryan, a burly Marylander who had volunteered as a private in the Confederate Army and, because of his peacetime vocation as a telegrapher, had naturally gravitated toward the signal service. Despite Alexander's condemnation of the enlisted men who worked for him, Bryan was far from stupid, and Alexander meant to use him to best advantage.

According to the plan, Bryan would go into Washington in civilian clothes and rent a room in sight of the Confederate-held hill across the Potomac. Bryan would indicate the room by placing a coffeepot on the window sill, where it could be seen through a powerful telescope that Alexander had obtained. Bryan would then begin to convey military information to Alexander from the Union's capital by manipulating the window blinds in certain prearranged ways.

Farfetched though the idea was, Alexander later insisted that it would have been "entirely feasible" had not General Joseph Johnston, by now in command of the Confederates around Manassas, pulled back beyond view of Washington's windows.

Disappointed but still determined, Alexander quickly set up an alternative system. Pliny Bryan was sent to a lonely spot on the Maryland side of the Potomac about 15 miles below Alexandria. There, through Confederate sympathizers who acted as couriers, he

I will not disclose, discover or use the plan for signals communicated to me, without the written consent of Dr. Myer & the consent of the U.S. War Department.

Edwd P Alexander
2nd Lt of Engrs
U.S. Army

In 1859, when Lieutenant Edward Porter Alexander helped test a primitive system of military signaling for the U.S. War Department, he wrote and signed a pledge of secrecy concerning the work. But at the outbreak of war, the pull of Southern loyalties proved stronger than his oath: The Georgia-born officer took the code of flag and torch signals with him when he joined the Confederate Army.

received messages and Northern newspaper clippings sent to him by an unidentified lady friend in Washington. Then, using Alexander's method of signaling, he transmitted the information to Confederates on the Virginia shore.

As sources of military intelligence, the Northern newspapers were especially useful. Although they sometimes were guilty of printing overly dramatic accounts of battles, the papers were also shockingly careless about security: They routinely carried accurate and detailed accounts of Union troop strengths and movements. From these newspaper columns Confederate officers were able to compile a list of Federal units in and around Washington, along with the names of their commanders, that was complete to the regimental level. Bryan's improvised arrangement worked well until the spring of 1862, when Federal authorities somehow

caught wind of his activities and arrested the big Marylander. By then, the versatile Porter Alexander had left Beauregard's signal service in other hands; he went on to become one of General Robert E. Lee's foremost artillerists.

Alexander's work while he was with Beauregard, however, had led to the establishment of a new department to serve the entire Army — the Confederate Army Signal Corps, made official by Congress in April of 1862. By the end of the summer, the new corps would have a special clandestine bureau whose assignments included espionage and whose head, Captain William Norris, was slated to become the Confederacy's chief spymaster.

From the beginning, the Secret Service Bureau operated as an arm of the War Department, but the bureau's ties with the individual Confederate Army commanders were complex and tenuous. Robert E. Lee was a general of the old school, who believed that wars should be waged by men wearing uniforms and bearing arms. He looked upon spying as a dirty affair with which he wanted as little to do as possible. "I have no confidence in any scout," he once said, using "scout" as a euphemism for "spy."

The Confederacy's main secret service therefore operated at a distance from Lee.

Major William Norris' espionage activities were distinguished from his duties as head of the Confederate Signal Bureau by the euphemistic phrase "special service." So secretive was the elusive major that many Confederate officials were unaware of his double role.

Coordination between Norris' organization and the commanding general was often lacking, and much of the information provided by the Secret Service Bureau was either ignored or scorned. What is more, many of Lee's generals — including James Longstreet and Jeb Stuart — tended to rely on their own spies, and in the resulting confusion it was not uncommon to find a single agent who worked sometimes for a field commander and on other occasions for Norris' Secret Service Bureau.

Given the confusion, it is remarkable that the bureau accomplished as much as it did. Many details of its role will probably never be known: By its very nature, the bureau operated in the shadows; moreover, most of its records were destroyed. Some documents were reportedly burned by Secretary of War Judah P. Benjamin to prevent them from falling into Federal hands as the War neared its end; other papers were consumed by the flames that finally engulfed Richmond.

Yet from the bits and pieces of evidence that remain, it seems clear that William Norris, starting with a collection of rank amateurs, many of whom had begun their espionage careers entirely on their own, somehow had been able to forge an organization of professionals who had ample cause for pride in their performance.

Norris was a tidy, bearded man who followed adventure but somehow blended into its background. The son of a Maryland hardware merchant, Norris graduated from Yale and then went to New Orleans to practice law. News of gold strikes in California, however, sent him hurrying west, and he arrived in San Francisco in March 1849, ahead of most of the forty-niners. But after considering his options, Norris shied away from the rough-and-tumble life of a gold prospector; instead, he found more congenial employment as a legal consultant for the U.S. Navy's Pacific Squadron.

After two years in California, Norris took a trip to Chile, then returned to Maryland and seemed to settle down. At 40, he had a delicate wife and five children — when the Civil War came along to offer a diversion.

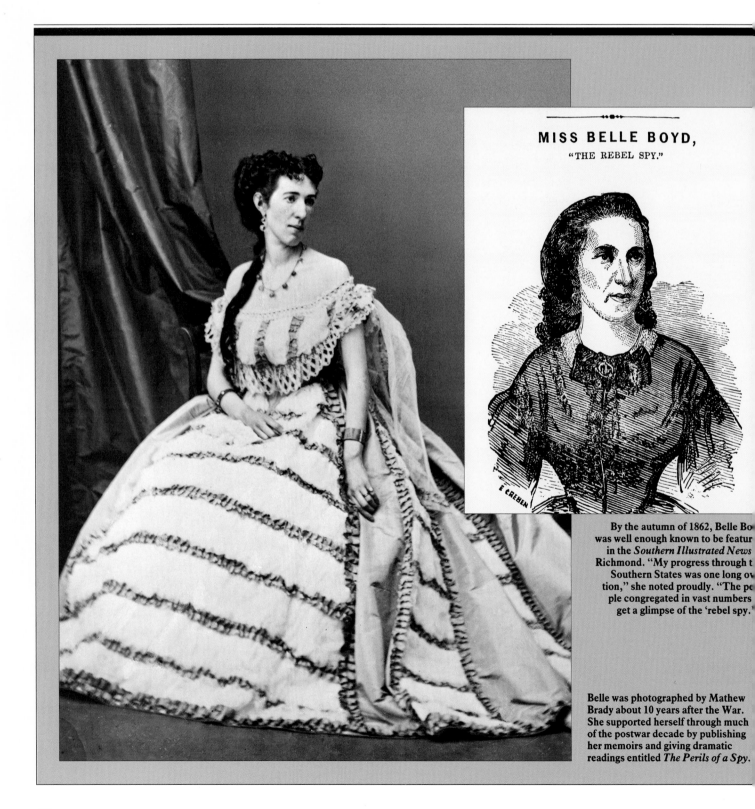

MISS BELLE BOYD,
"THE REBEL SPY."

By the autumn of 1862, Belle Bo
was well enough known to be featur
in the *Southern Illustrated News*
Richmond. "My progress through t
Southern States was one long ov
tion," she noted proudly. "The pe
ple congregated in vast numbers
get a glimpse of the 'rebel spy.'

Belle was photographed by Mathew
Brady about 10 years after the War.
She supported herself through much
of the postwar decade by publishing
her memoirs and giving dramatic
readings entitled *The Perils of a Spy*.

The Siren of the Shenandoah

"From the force of circumstances," wrote Belle Boyd, "and not through any desire of my own, I became a celebrity." In fact, she became the most famous female spy of the Civil War, and arguably the least effective.

Daughter of a Shenandoah Valley farmer and merchant, Belle was a spirited teenager who saw the War as personal drama. In 1861 she became a Confederate courier, running messages and medicine through the Union lines. Two exploits, she asserted, made her famous. When Union troops occupied her hometown of Martinsburg, Belle killed a soldier who insulted her mother. Later, she provided General Stonewall Jackson with intelligence that led to his surprise attack on Union forces at Front Royal, Virginia. Jackson wrote thanking her on behalf of the Army, she said — although no one ever saw the letter.

Belle was arrested six times, imprisoned twice and reported more times than her neighbors could remember. Her problem was not lack of brains but love of publicity. She talked incessantly about her real or imagined exploits, preferably to reporters. The grateful press called her "the Siren of the Shenandoah," "the Rebel Joan of Arc," "the Secesh Cleopatra." After her final arrest, late in the War, Union authorities lost patience with the spy and deported her to neutral Canada.

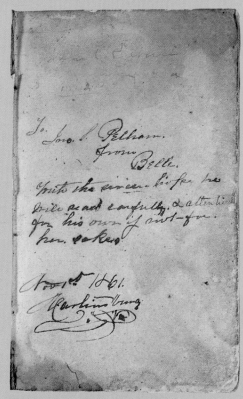

Dedicated in Belle's hand to the dashing Alabama artillery officer John Pelham, this Bible became a valued relic after Pelham's death.

Dressed in Confederate gray and wearing a hat popularized by Jeb Stuart, Belle filled theaters in the North and South after the War.

Volunteering to serve for the Confederacy in 1861, Norris became a civilian aide on the staff of General John Magruder on Virginia's Peninsula. Evidently thinking that Norris' work for the Navy had given him some experience with communications, Magruder placed him in charge of his command's signal operations with the rank of captain. In those early months of the War, Norris was apparently unfamiliar with Porter Alexander's flag-waving method, and so he devised his own system, which used flags and colored balls that were run up and down on poles.

Although Norris' method was not as sophisticated as Alexander's, it was good enough to impress Confederate authorities, and in the spring of 1862 Norris was posted with the new Confederate Army Signal Corps in Richmond. By July 1862 he had established, as a covert organization of the

Signal Corps, the Secret Service Bureau.

Sharing a building with the Signal Corps on Richmond's Capitol Square, the Secret Service came to include 10 captains, 20 lieutenants, 30 sergeants and scores of enlisted men from the ranks of army regiments.

"These men," wrote one of the officers, "when occasion required, became dauntless messengers and agents, going into the enemy's lines and cities; communicating with agents and secret friends of the Confederate Government; ordering supplies and conveying them to their destination; making nightly voyages in bays and rivers; threading the enemy's cordon of pickets and gunboats; following blind trails through swamp and forest; and as much experts with oar and sail, on deck and in the saddle, and with rifle and revolver, as with flags, torches, and secret cipher."

A sketch by Dr. A. J. Volck, a Baltimore dentist who doubled as a Confederate courier, shows a small boat laden with contraband running across the Potomac. A shell fired from a Federal picket post on the Maryland shore splashes in the water off the boat's portside.

Although their activities eventually extended into Canada, Norris' agents focused their main attentions on the Union's capital — and on the Potomac River lines of clandestine communication that had, as a phenomenon of civil war, existed almost since the start of the conflict.

For two centuries, the inhabitants of northern Virginia and southern Maryland had shared familial, social, business and political interests. For these Americans, the Potomac River had served not as a dividing line but as a concourse for communications. In the passions aroused by all the prewar oratory, little thought had been given to such practical considerations as postal service in a divided nation — and of all the War's inconveniences, perhaps none so outraged the Marylanders and Virginians as the fact that their normal intercourse, especially the mail, was cut off.

From frustration it was a short step to smuggling, and before long, boats — some of them with plugs in the bottom so that the vessels could be submerged and hidden when not in use — were setting out in the dark of night, bearing messages and other contraband, from the inlets of such Potomac tributaries as Port Tobacco River, Pope's Creek and Gunston Cove. At first, most of the couriers were mere boys who made the trip as a lark. But as Federal picket boats began patrolling the river, more-seasoned hands took over the networks — or, as they were called, lines — with remarkably efficient results. New York newspapers, for example, could be collected in Washington, carried by horseback to Pope's Creek, ferried across the Potomac and taken by road to Port Royal on the Rappahannock; from Port Royal they were taken across the river and

carried the final 18 miles to Richmond, sometimes reaching the city within 24 hours of their publication.

Shortly after William Norris, by now a Confederate major, set up his Secret Service Bureau, he wrote a letter explaining that one of his agency's main duties would be to take over "the management and supplying of secret lines of communications on the Potomac." To that end, a lieutenant named Charles H. Cawood, who had already shown a knack for crossing the Potomac, was placed in charge of a permanent station on the Virginia bank — just across the river from the 540-acre Maryland farm of Thomas A. Jones, a key link in Norris' network.

Jones was one of thousands of ordinary Marylanders who were caught up in the human conflicts of civil war in a border state. When the War began, Jones's home, about 40 miles south of Washington on a high bluff near Pope's Creek, became a stopping place for southbound strangers who for various reasons wished to get across the river. There the river narrowed — although it was still more than a mile wide — and the crossing was the shortest and quickest along that length of the Potomac. As a Southern sympathizer, Jones at first accommodated travelers without charge, rowing them across in the small boat in which he had idled away many peacetime hours fishing for shad. Then, as the traffic increased, he had begun to collect a fare of one dollar per person.

That modest enterprise came to an end in September 1861, when Federal troops, after questioning a black youth who sometimes helped Jones, arrested the farmer and clapped him into the Old Capitol Prison, where he remained for several months before being freed at the urging of his Congressman. During Jones's incarceration his wife had died — and for that, rightly or wrongly, Thomas A. Jones blamed the Union.

It was therefore a timely coincidence that, several months after his release, Jones should receive a visit from Major William Norris, who was on the prowl for locations that could be used as signal posts and safehouses for traveling Confederate agents. Upon first viewing Jones's property, Norris exclaimed, "What a place this would be for a signal station!" And so it was: From its clifftop position nearly 100 feet above the Potomac, Jones's house commanded a view of a nine-mile stretch of the river, and from that vantage point, Federal patrol boats could easily be spotted.

Thirsting for revenge against the Federal powers that he believed responsible for his wife's death, Jones agreed to Norris' request that he maintain a regular ferrying service for Confederate messages and agents. He fully realized the risk involved — he had already been arrested once, and the Federals would be watching him.

"It required great caution and unrelaxing vigilance," Jones said later. In addition to the Union gunboats that roved up and down the Potomac during the daylight hours, patrols from a nearby Union post visited Jones's place sporadically, and Union pickets were stationed along the Maryland bluffs. Yet Jones knew that at dusk the shadows cast by the hills on the Virginia side reached almost across the Potomac, making small craft difficult to see. Moreover, Jones had also observed that Federal pickets did not come on duty along the river until dark.

It was thus relatively safe for a boat to cross the river quickly at dusk. If any Federals were in the vicinity of the Jones farm, a Maryland-bound boatman was warned away by a black cloth hung in the attic window of a neighbor's house, also atop the bluff and clearly visible from the Virginia side. Once across, the boatman would debark a passenger or deposit packets from Richmond in the fork of a dead tree, pick up any southbound messages or agents and row back unseen.

After the Federal pickets went off duty the next morning, Jones would stroll down to the tree and pick up and sort through the delivery; he sent most of the mail northward by the simple expedient of dropping it off at a nearby post office and letting the Federal postal system do the rest of the Confeder-

To Muzzle an Unbridled Press

Most Confederate generals were assiduous readers of contraband Northern newspapers, from which they learned much about Union strategy and strength. Thus General Lee, on April 30, 1864, was able to write to President Jefferson Davis: "I send you the Philadelphia *Inquirer* of the 26th, from which you will learn that all Burnside's available forces are being advanced to the front." Northern generals knew of the problem, and they raged about press leaks that many thought amounted to treason.

The problem was peculiarly Northern, for the South had far fewer papers. The Federal government could not censor the hundreds of correspondents, including scores from abroad, who covered the War from Washington and in the field. Although commanders imposed their own censorship at times — often to hide official ineptitude — they accomplished little.

Yet while many news dispatches undoubtedly aided the Confederates, others were too inaccurate to constitute a threat. The less scrupulous correspondents fabricated eyewitness accounts of battles they never saw, and even the better papers, li[ke] the New York *Herald*, printed war maps [so] fanciful that they were mockingly com[pared by those in the know to "pictures o[f a] drunkard's stomach."

Reporting improved as the War pr[o]gressed, but the temper of commanders d[id] not. General William Tecumseh Sherm[an] had one correspondent tried as a spy — [he] was acquitted — and General Ambro[se] Burnside ordered a New York *Times* r[e]porter shot. General Ulysses S. Grant cou[n]termanded that order — perhaps aware th[at] leaks began with the military. "If I ha[ve] watermelons and whiskey ready when of[fi]cers come along from a fight," said the Ne[w] York *Tribune's* Charles Page, "I get th[e] news without asking questions."

War correspondents and artists [of] the Boston *Herald* and oth[er] newspapers share a seasonal toa[st] at Christmas in 1864. The fame[d] *Harper's* artist Alfred Waud [is] seated second from the righ[t]

acy's work for him. More urgent messages, however, he entrusted to members of the so-called Doctors' Line, comprising secessionist physicians. Since their calling kept them out at all hours, the doctors could move at will without suspicion, aided by medical bags that served as unofficial passports. One of the line's leading figures was Dr. Stowton Dent, of whom Jones recalled: "The number of papers he could conceal in his pockets and boot legs was astonishing."

Among those who used the Doctors' Line and the Jones-Cawood facilities was an extraordinary Confederate agent named Thomas Nelson Conrad — who, like nearly all the spies of the Civil War, moved without an iota of training from tranquil peacetime pursuits to one of the most perilous of wartime occupations.

In June 1861, commencement exercises were held at Georgetown College, a private preparatory school across Rock Creek from the rest of Washington. As the ceremonies ended, a band struck up "Dixie." Southern ladies in the audience, wrote the college's headmaster, "stood upon chairs, frantically waving their handkerchiefs" while "cheer after cheer sounded through the hall."

That very evening, Georgetown's head-

master, Thomas Nelson Conrad, was arrested, clapped into irons and marched off to the Old Capitol Prison by a squad of Union soldiers. Charged, among other allegations, with sending recruits from his school to the Confederate Army, Conrad was subsequently taken to Fort Monroe in Virginia, whence he was sent to Richmond in exchange for a Federal prisoner.

Although Conrad had graduated from Dickinson College in Pennsylvania, he was a born-and-bred Virginian, and he had lost none of his love for the South. Now, after a whiff of Federal jails, he was, as he put it, "on the warpath." No sooner had he been freed than he hastened to Culpeper, Virginia, where the Confederacy's Major General Jeb Stuart had established his cavalry headquarters. By chance, the first officer Conrad ran into was the Rev. Major Dabney Ball, head chaplain of Stuart's cavalry corps. Learning that Conrad was seeking military employment, Ball suggested that he become a chaplain. And so, although he had never been more than a lay reader in the Methodist Church, he did.

Assigned to the 3rd Virginia Cavalry Regiment, Conrad assumed his clerical duties with, as he put it, "enthusiastic ardor and burning zeal." But though he proved to be a spirited sermonizer on such militant subjects as "The Christian Soldier" and "David, a Mighty Warrior," he soon realized that the chaplaincy was not his forte. Instead, Conrad found that he preferred the life of a scout, and he began riding out alone on reconnaissance missions. On occasion, he donned a "straight-breasted coat of black cloth" and discovered that in the guise of a Northern clergyman, he could move more or less at will around enemy camps.

In a photograph for his wife, Southern spy Henry Thomas Harrison, in a lieutenant's uniform, points to a coded message meaning "I love you." General James Longstreet judged Harrison's reports about Union troop movements "more accurate than a force of cavalry could have secured."

After several months of such enterprises, Conrad was summoned to the War Department in Richmond for "special duty." Conrad's mission was to go to Washington and bring back two European emissaries, one British and the other French, who were in the United States to discuss with the Confederates a possible loan of three million dollars. What finally happened to the deal is unknown. What is certain is that Conrad successfully got the diplomats through the Union's porous Potomac lines and then returned to the Federal capital, where he spent

much of the remainder of the War as a spy.

Conrad's qualifications were impressive: He had already shown a proclivity for secret doings; from his days as an educator he was familiar with the city; and as a former inmate of the Old Capitol he could be expected to take every precaution against being returned to its confines. Worried lest he be recognized, Conrad changed the styling of his beard from its original full growth to the side-whisker cut favored by General Ambrose Burnside and, later, to a thick mustache and a short, pointed beard called an imperial. From the homemade plantation riding boots prevalent in the South, Conrad switched to the machine-manufactured kind that were generally worn in the North. And instead of the plug tobacco popular in the South, he chewed the shredded variety that was favored by Northerners.

As a first order of business in Washington, Conrad established himself in patrician comfort in a mansion built in the early 1800s by the wealthy and politically prominent General John Peter Van Ness and now owned by one Thomas Green, a secret supporter of the South. The place was perfect for Conrad's purposes: Convenient to the Federal War Department, it was surrounded by a high brick wall whose entrance was guarded by a porter's lodge, where unwelcome visitors could be turned away.

Safely ensconced, Conrad set about organizing an espionage ring. From his earlier days in Washington, he knew of some War Department clerks whose loyalties lay with the South. "These I met by appointment and talked over the situation with them," he wrote later. "They were ready to serve me and the cause I represented with gladness."

The arrangement soon paid off. During McClellan's Peninsular Campaign in 1862, one of Conrad's War Department agents had access to the Union order of battle. The figures were duly stolen, and in the weeks that followed, similar reports evidently came to Conrad, enabling him to write later that throughout the Union army's advance up the Peninsula, authorities in Richmond "knew just what forces McClellan had, down to the exact number of pieces of artillery."

Bold and even reckless when he deemed it necessary, Conrad was ordinarily a prudent sort of spy. To avoid running into people who might recognize him, he stayed out of hotel lobbies, restaurants and saloons. When he felt in need of divine guidance, Methodist Conrad attended Catholic services where he was certain he would meet no one who knew him. Rendezvous with his agents usually took place at night and — presumably on the notion that a public building would be the last place Federal authorities would suspect of being a meeting place for Confederate spies — often on the steps of the Interior Department.

The South's Bumbling Spycatcher

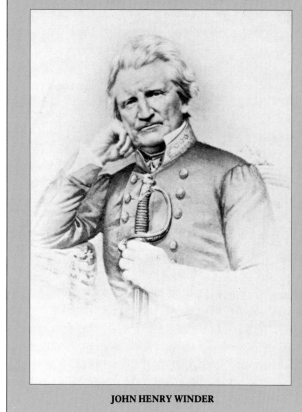

JOHN HENRY WINDER

One of the more ineffectual operators in the clandestine wars was John Henry Winder, the provost marshal of Richmond and thereby the Confederacy's chief of counterespionage. Although the baleful old brigadier general apprehended a few spies — most notably the unfortunate Pinkerton agent, Timothy Webster — many more Union agents operated freely in the Confederate capital.

Winder's main handicaps as a spycatcher were his near-total ignorance of espionage and his eager mendacity. His palm, it was widely believed, remained open to receive illicit payments. The brown-paper travel passes essential for moving about the Confederacy could be had for $100 apiece. One Union spy recalled getting the permit he needed by making a generous contribution for Winder to buy a full-dress uniform.

The provost marshal's detective force was composed mostly of untrained rowdies. His headquarters was made "repulsive by the smell of whiskey," said a visitor — and security was nonexistent. One day guards chased but failed to catch a stranger they found jotting down notes before a headquarters wall. There, by Winder's eccentric orders, were chalked the names and strengths of all Confederate regiments defending the Peninsula southeast of Richmond.

Beyond such precautions, Conrad scored a major coup by forestalling the efforts of the man most likely to catch him — Colonel Lafayette Baker, head of the U.S. War Department's secret police force.

Baker, a lean, muscular New Yorker with flinty gray eyes, held the rank of colonel and the title of special provost marshal for the War Department. Earlier in the War, he had spied for the Union, traveling through the South and even gaining an audience with Jefferson Davis — or so he claimed.

As a spycatcher, Baker had a reputation for utter ruthlessness. During his regime, citizens disappeared from their homes in the night; so many prisoners were held, often without formal charges being filed against them, that they filled Carroll Prison, an annex of the Old Capitol.

To escape the clutches of Lafayette Baker, Thomas Conrad devised an elaborate scheme. Shortly after he took up residence in Washington, Conrad arranged to have a Confederate enlisted man pretend to desert, make his way to Washington and present himself to Baker as an embittered Southerner who desired to work for the Union as a counterespionage agent. "His name was Edward Norton," Conrad later explained; "he was a brave young fellow with no end of brass

Lafayette Baker, head of the Federal secret police, stands before Jefferson Davis during his purported audience with the Confederate President in Richmond. In his lurid account of the meeting, Baker maintained that he concealed his identity as a spy from both Davis and Georgia politician Robert Toombs, who lay on a sofa "looking like a man who had imbibed too freely."

and self-assurance." Incredibly, Baker took the bait, and, according to Conrad, the "upshot of it all was that Norton received an appointment as one of Colonel Baker's most trusted detectives."

Conrad's success in placing his double agent on Baker's force undoubtedly saved his life. Sometime in mid-1863, Norton warned Conrad that Baker was aware of his activities and was hot on his heels. Assigning Norton to run affairs in his absence, Conrad hastily fled from Washington—and when, less than an hour after Conrad's departure, Baker's men raided the Van Ness mansion, they came away empty-handed.

The exact auspices under which Conrad had so far been operating are by no means clear. Although he surely acted some of the time on direct orders from the Confederate War De-

partment, on other occasions he apparently received his spying assignments from Jeb Stuart. At least once he returned to his old regiment, where he was "glad to learn that the Christian associations I had formed in the regiment had continued their religious services." It is probable, however, that within a short time after his narrow escape from Washington, Captain Thomas Nelson Conrad began working for Major William Norris and the Confederate Secret Service Bureau.

At any rate, with Washington temporarily closed to him, Conrad now repaired to Boyd's Hole on the Virginia bank of the lower Potomac, 35 miles from Washington, where he had determined to build what he called "my wigwam." The wigwam turned out to be a shanty that Conrad named the Eagle Nest (an eagle did, in fact, have a nest in a nearby tree); it was built high on a cliff overlooking the river. He acquired a little keel-bottomed boat that he dubbed the *Rebel Queen,* along with three good horses, a pocket compass and a high-powered field glass. Assisted by two couriers and a pair of Irish oarsmen, Conrad was quickly back in business, receiving information from other agents in the North, assisting in the passage of couriers, and helping to move valuable contraband goods into the Confederacy.

Although he was keenly aware that "Baker's bloodhounds were scenting in every quarter for my trail," Conrad nonetheless returned several times to Washington. And in March of 1864, shortly before Ulysses S. Grant, newly named commander of all the Union armies, plunged into Virginia's Wilderness to open the campaign that led eventually to Appomattox, Conrad undertook an especially hazardous journey to Annapolis.

There, 25,000 men of Ambrose Burnside's IX Corps were massing for reasons that Confederate authorities longed to learn. Was Burnside preparing to join Grant in a Virginia offensive? Or was he about to embark on a coastal expedition farther south, as he had successfully done in early 1862? Wearing his old clergyman's outfit, Conrad went to Annapolis and, as he said, "walked all over and around that ancient borough; inside and outside the Naval Academy grounds; talked with gentlemen about the hotels, and particularly with a bright clerk in one of the leading hotels."

Conrad was soon able to send a message to Richmond: "Burnside will reinforce Grant, and that at an early day." Sure enough, that was exactly what Burnside did. Forewarned of the Federal movement, General Lee was able to prepare with greater certainty his plans for the Battle of the Wilderness.

Colonel Benjamin Sweet took command of Camp Douglas after a severe wound left him unfit for active duty.

Missions From Canada

As the tide of war turned against the Confederacy in 1864, a clandestine force of experienced military men laid plans to cripple the Union from within. Based in Canada, the Confederates plotted to strike across the border in a series of raids beginning in late August with the liberation of Illinois' Camp Douglas, where 10,000 Confederate prisoners of war were confined. Then, with an inmate army, the leaders planned to march on Chicago to disrupt the Democratic National Convention. There, it was hoped, thousan[s] of sympathizers such as the antiwar Coppe[r]heads would join their cause. The raiders f[u]ly expected to have 50,000 men movi[ng] across the Northwest states in 10 days.

This grandiose plan — which include[d] seizing the governments of Illinois, India[na] and Ohio — was thwarted by the command[er] of Camp Douglas, Colonel Benjamin Swe[et]. Learning of the plot while censoring pris[on] mail, Sweet quickly strengthened his gar[rison]

n. Somehow alerted, the Confederates can-
led their raid. But they planned a second
ack for November — this time joined by
ieutenant James Shanks, a recent escapee
om Camp Douglas. Before the attempt
uld be made, however, the leaders were
rested in Chicago: Shanks, it turned out,
as a Union spy.

The scheme to liberate Camp Douglas fiz-
ed, but many of the Confederates who es-
ped arrest were already at work on the next
ase of their operations, a plot to attack
Northern town.

Confederate prisoners mill
about Camp Douglas while
Union soldiers stand guard
in the foreground. A contemporary newspaper mused on
the consequences of a prison
breakout: "The country
through which they bent
their way would be devastat-
ed by pillage, incendiarism,
rapine and all the horrors
which can be imagined."

As the Confederate Commissioner,
to Canada, Jacob Thompson (above)
planned the Camp Douglas plot;
Tom Hines (left), a dashing cavalry
captain noted for his resemblance
to the actor John Wilkes Booth,
was to lead the actual raid.

The Raid on St. Albans

The place the Confederates decided to attack was St. Albans, Vermont, a small town conveniently located only 20 miles south of the Canadian border. The plan was to seize and burn St. Albans and, if time allowed, rob its banks.

On October 15, 1864, Lieutenant Bennett Young and his 25 raiders casually drifted into St. Albans wearing civilian clothes, found lodging and began to scout the town. Young, by all accounts a charming and witty man, even squired a local young woman around town to evaluate the village green as a potential holding area for prisoners without arousing suspicion.

On October 19 the raiders met at the edge of town. At 3 p.m. Young mounted a stolen horse and led his men toward the green. Brandishing a pistol, he attracted the attention of passersby and then declared, "Gentlemen, I am a Confederate officer. I've come to take your town and I'm going to do it." It is not surprising, since the nearest battleground was 400 miles away, that Young's announcement was greeted with disbelief and even laughter, but a few shots fired over the Vermonters' heads soon convinced them of the gravity of the situation. Then, in a reversal of priorities that later cast a shadow on the raid, the Confederates set at once to robbing the town's three banks. Even in this, Young displayed a

Main Street in St. Albans, Vermont, appears pleasant and placid in a photograph taken around the time that Bennett Young and his men staged their raid on the town.

Young's raiders hold a bewildered teller at gunpoint as they rob the St. Albans Bank on the afternoon of October 19, 1864.

certain *élan:* In the Bank of St. Albans he ordered an elderly teller at gunpoint to remain "immutably fixed" to his chair until released — a month later Young would send word to the old man that his "term of service is now expired."

The raiders were soon put to flight by citizens led by a Union cavalry captain who was home on leave. By then Young's men had set fire to the town, although the flames sputtered out with little damage done. The Confederates fled into Canada where most of them, including Young, were captured by local authorities and underwent trials and extradition procedures that stretched well past the end of the War. None of the raiders were ever sentenced for their deeds.

After St. Albans, only a few Confederates remained free in Canada to carry out the final — and most desperate — phase of their operations.

The horsemen of a Vermont posse (*foreground*) are temporarily stymied by a blazing covered bridge set afire by the raiders. The chase resumed within minutes, however, and continued into Canada, where the raiders were taken into custody.

Six raiders appear proud in a photograph taken in a Montreal jail. Lieutenant Bennett Young, their leader, is seated at right.

Assault on New York City

By Election Day of 1864, the so-called Canadian operations had proved a series of dismal failures. The plots had all crumbled, and expected popular support in the North had never materialized. In the face of these frustrations, a group of six determined Confederates headed by Lieutenant John W. Headley went ahead with a mission — to burn the city of New York in "one dazzling conflagration."

The six saboteurs slipped into New York, each equipped with 10 bottles of a flammable phosphorous liquid known as Greek fire. Each of the six men took rooms in three or four different hotels across the city. At dusk on November 25, the raiders set to work. Going from hotel to hotel, each man piled mattresses and linens on the floor of the room that he had rented, then doused everything with Greek fire. In all, the act was repeated in 19 hotels across the city, but the Greek fire proved unreliable. Those fires that did catch were quickly contained, and the rest smoldered and sputtered out, leaving city authorities free to turn their whole attention to capturing the Confederates. One man was caught and hanged; the others managed to board a train and get away. In the end the raiders had caused a great deal of excitement but little damage, and their defiant plot, like the entire Canadian operation, had been a proud but empty effort.

The glow of a match illuminates this Confederate's fiendish sneer in a fanciful illustration from a Northern newspaper. Actually, if the Confederates had used matches instead of the unreliable Greek fire, their plan might have succeeded.

After his brief but significant trip to Annapolis, Conrad returned to his Potomac hideaway and resumed his former activities. By late 1864, his efforts had left him completely frazzled. "The nerve-exhausting drain had well nigh prostrated me," he later recalled. "Another week of such ceaseless excitement would likely have placed me hors de combat." Traveling to Richmond, Conrad was converted from spy to counterspy and given instructions to nab Federal agents who were known to be operating in the Confederate capital.

For the rest of the War, Conrad was engaged in counterespionage, with a notable lack of success. For him, the exhilarating yet nerve-wearing days of spying were over. But even after Lee's surrender at Appomattox, there remained for Conrad a moment of high drama. In his most recent tonsorial change he had shaved his beard and adopted the mustache and hairstyle of one of the most popular young actors of the day. And so it happened that Thomas Nelson Conrad, while returning to the North to seek a peacetime vocation, was arrested in Maryland — and held until he could prove that his name was not John Wilkes Booth, for whom a nationwide manhunt was under way as the assassin of Abraham Lincoln.

During much of the time that Conrad had been active as a spy, the enigmatic Major William Norris had pulled not only his strings but had directed many other Southern agents as well. Scattered references to Norris' activities as the Confederacy's chief spymaster pop up here and there in various documents (once, for example, his request to the War Department for $200 a month to finance the operations of the Potomac couriers was approved), and it is known that for about 10 months in 1864 Norris was on a mysterious mission that took him to the embattled regions of the Deep South.

Beyond these notations, almost nothing can be found. Neither then nor later did Norris go beyond the vaguest references in explaining the role he had played in the War. Not only were the records of the secret service destroyed by fire, but nearly all of Norris' personal papers were lost when his Maryland home burned in 1890. His death in 1896 attracted little attention, and he was quickly forgotten.

Norris' work went unappreciated as well. Indeed, the few references to Norris in General Robert E. Lee's wartime papers mostly dismissed his efforts. On April 27, 1863, the day before the Union's General Joseph Hooker began to cross the Rappahannock River on his way to Chancellorsville, Lee had written James Longstreet, who was on detached duty in southeast Virginia. Norris, Lee said, had estimated Hooker's strength at more than 150,000 men and had reported that at least 10,000 Union reinforcements were on their way to confront Longstreet. Then Lee added: "I think his statement very much exaggerated."

In fact, Hooker had more than 130,000 effectives at Chancellorsville, and nearly 9,000 men were on their way to face Longstreet. Norris' estimates were therefore well within acceptable ranges and provided ample evidence that, within a year after starting almost from scratch, William Norris and his spies were performing valuable service — with little recognition from the generals whose cause they served.

Making War with Codes and Ciphers

In July of 1861, when Major Albert J. Myer was ordered to organize a Signal Corps for the U.S. Army, he immediately recognized a critical problem: how to keep messages from the prying eyes and ears of the enemy. To use a standard and unchanging system of flag signals would advertise important information to every Confederate within eyesight. Similarly, the electric telegraph, just then coming into widespread use, employed a worldwide code of dots and dashes to transmit messages; enemy agents and scouts could tap in at any point along the thousands of miles of unguarded wires and read off the communications with ease.

The solution, of course, was to use secret code — to encipher all messages, both signal-flag and telegraphic, in a way that would befuddle the watching and listening enemy. Both sides hastened to devise ingenious codes and ciphers, some of which are shown on these pages. Once encoded, an intercepted message held scant value to the enemy — unless he had succeeded in breaking the code.

With his signal flags propped behind him, a Union signal officer peers through his telescope, ready to receive a message.

A.J.M.

No._____

Cipher disks like this were used by Federal soldiers to encode signal-flag messages. The numbers on the outer ring denote standard flag movements that represent the letters on the inner ring. By turning the rings according to a prearranged setting, signalmen could change the code at will. Myer thought these disks so sensitive that he urged his men to sacrifice their lives rather than allow the disks to fall into Confederate hands.

This transcription of a telegraph message from Major Thomas Eckert, Superintendent of the U.S. Military Telegraph, attests to the Union's growing concern for secrecy.

Union signalmen wave their flag from atop a signal tower in Bermuda Hundred, Virginia. Such lofty platforms made signals visible at a great distance.

USING THE CYPHER

EXAMPLE:

Sentence	—	SEND	MORE	AMMUNITION
Key	—	LIBE	RTYO	RDEATHLIBE
Cypher	—	DMOH	DHPS	RPQUGPEQPR

TRANSLATING THE CYPHER

Cypher	—	DMOH	DHPS	RPQUGPEQPR
Key	—	LIBE	RTYO	RDEATHLIBE
Sentence	—	SEND	MORE	AMMUNITION

The example above shows the workings of the Confederate cipher. The key — "Liberty or death" — has been written out below the plaintext message and repeated until each letter of the plain text has a corresponding key letter. To encipher the message, find its first letter — *S* — in the first row of the square at right. Then find the first letter of the cipher key — *L* — in the first column. The point at which the column and row converge yields the cipher letter — *D*. To translate the enciphered message, locate the first letter of the cipher key — *L* — in the first column of the square. Follow that row out to the first letter of the cipher text — *D*. Now follow that column up to the top of the square to arrive at *S*, the first letter of the actual message.

```
A B C D E F G H I J K L M N O P Q R S T U V W X Y Z
B C D E F G H I J K L M N O P Q R S T U V W X Y Z A
C D E F G H I J K L M N O P Q R S T U V W X Y Z A B
D E F G H I J K L M N O P Q R S T U V W X Y Z A B C
E F G H I J K L M N O P Q R S T U V W X Y Z A B C D
F G H I J K L M N O P Q R S T U V W X Y Z A B C D E
G H I J K L M N O P Q R S T U V W X Y Z A B C D E F
H I J K L M N O P Q R S T U V W X Y Z A B C D E F G
I J K L M N O P Q R S T U V W X Y Z A B C D E F G H
J K L M N O P Q R S T U V W X Y Z A B C D E F G H I
K L M N O P Q R S T U V W X Y Z A B C D E F G H I J
L M N O P Q R S T U V W X Y Z A B C D E F G H I J K
M N O P Q R S T U V W X Y Z A B C D E F G H I J K L
N O P Q R S T U V W X Y Z A B C D E F G H I J K L M
O P Q R S T U V W X Y Z A B C D E F G H I J K L M N
P Q R S T U V W X Y Z A B C D E F G H I J K L M N O
Q R S T U V W X Y Z A B C D E F G H I J K L M N O P
R S T U V W X Y Z A B C D E F G H I J K L M N O P Q
S T U V W X Y Z A B C D E F G H I J K L M N O P Q R
T U V W X Y Z A B C D E F G H I J K L M N O P Q R S
U V W X Y Z A B C D E F G H I J K L M N O P Q R S T
V W X Y Z A B C D E F G H I J K L M N O P Q R S T U
W X Y Z A B C D E F G H I J K L M N O P Q R S T U V
X Y Z A B C D E F G H I J K L M N O P Q R S T U V W
Y Z A B C D E F G H I J K L M N O P Q R S T U V W
Z A B C D E F G H I J K L M N O P Q R S T U V W X
  C D E F G H I J K L M N O P Q R S T U V W X Y
```

When a cipher square similar to this one was found among the effects of John Wilkes Booth, outraged Unionists tried to link President Lincoln's assassination to the Confederate government. Actually, the square was familiar to both sides; a more convincing piece of evidence would have been a proven Confederate cipher key.

This brass disk was an alternative to the cipher square. To encode each letter of a message, first the inner wheel of the disk was turned to line up a key letter with the letter *A* on the outer wheel. Then the operator located the appropriate message letter on the outer wheel and, beneath it on the inner wheel, found the code letter.

The Quest for Concealment

The need for secure codes was doubly urgent for the Confederates, who could not string their own military telegraph wire and were forced to rely on civilian companies. With little cryptographic experience, the Confederates pressed into service a 400-year-old European system known as the "court" or "diplomatic" cipher.

The results were mixed. Though the code was difficult to crack, the complex letter-by-letter encipherment and the normal margin of telegraphic error frequently led to garbled messages. After spending 12 hours trying to decipher a message, one Confederate officer got on his horse, rode all the way around the Union flank and approached the sender directly to find out what he had meant to say.

The solution to the Confederate cipher hinged on a predetermined key word or phrase. One of the more commonly used keys was "Complete Victory," but near war's end, when all hope of victory had vanished, a new cipher key came into use. Two weeks after Lee's surrender, President Jefferson Davis sent the last official cryptogram of the Confederacy, using as his key "Come Retribution."

Though Union signalmen sometimes boasted of their ease in breaking the Confederate cipher, this decoded message from Confederate General John Pemberton at Vicksburg suggests otherwise. The third word has been incorrectly translated as "caution," which does not even have the right number of letters. The actual word was "Canton."

Cracking a Cryptogram

While intercepting a coded telegraph message was easily done, breaking its code was quite another matter. In Washington, three energetic young telegraphers named David Bates, Charles Tinker and Albert Chandler puzzled over, and sometimes solved, various Confederate codes — often under the watchful eye of President Lincoln himself.

Confederate operators were equally persistent, if less successful, at breaking codes. Charles Gaston spent two months listening in on Federal communications, only to hear an impenetrable flow of cipher. But once, a Federal quartermaster neglected to use a code when telegraphing the location of a herd of beef cattle. Gaston sent the message straight to General Lee, and Confederate raiders captured the herd.

Telegraph operators' keys like this Milliken Repeater were used by both sides in telegraph offices and in field headquarters, but the machines were too bulky to be used for wiretapping.

While a courier stands by, the Union's Chief Signal Officer, Albert J. Myer, prepares a message in a tent near the front during the Second Bull Run Campaign in 1862.

A signalman in civilian garb clings to the top of a telegraph pole, ready to test or repair the wires. A pocket-size key like the one above was used for this purpose. Though awkward, pocket keys could also be used to tap wires to intercept messages or to send false ones.

The Message behind Meaningless Words

"Crimea both reserves even were that all the repulsed . . . ." Thus began a message from General George B. McClellan to Washington during the Seven Days battles in June 1862. The dispatch (in its entirety, right) had been encoded in what was called Route Transposition Cipher, the system favored by the Union Signal Corps.

To use the route cipher, the intended plain-text message was written across a set of columns (below, right). Null, or meaningless, words were included to fill out the matrix, and certain sensitive words, such as "attack," were replaced with code words — in this case, "oyster." Then the message was transcribed by following a predetermined route up and down the columns to yield an unintelligible string of words that could be transmitted safely over the telegraph. In the McClellan report, the route travels up the fourth column, down the third, up the fifth and so on to produce the message on the right.

The system reduced telegraphic error.

Because the Federals' encoded messages used recognizable words rather than the apparently random sequences of letters found in the Confederates' enciphered messages, telegraphers were less likely to misread the text. By tapping wires, the Confederates got innumerable samples of the Federals' route cipher, but they were unable to crack it. They published some of the enciphered messages in Southern newspapers and sought a solution from the public, but none was ever forthcoming.

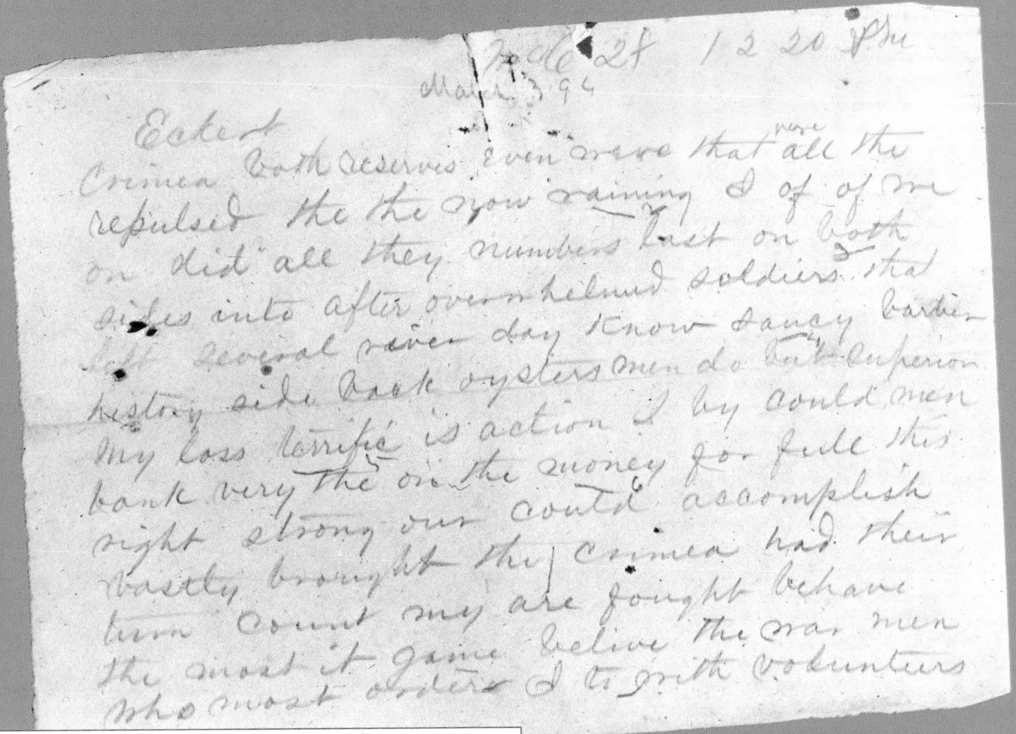

Eckert

June 28 1 2 20 PM
March 94

(handwritten draft dispatch — a jumble of words)

Cipher books, like this one (*left*) belonging to William R. Plum of the Military Telegraph Corps, were the road maps of the route cipher. They contained instructions and route patterns for working out enciphered messages.

This seemingly nonsensical jumble of words (*above*) was telegraphed by General McClellan to Secretary of War Stanton on June 28, 1862. The first word — Crimea — was a codeword indicating the number of columns and the number of words in each column necessary to decipher the message. At left is the message routed through six columns according to a prescribed pattern. The dispatch may now be understood simply by reading across the columns in normal sentences, starting from the top of the page.

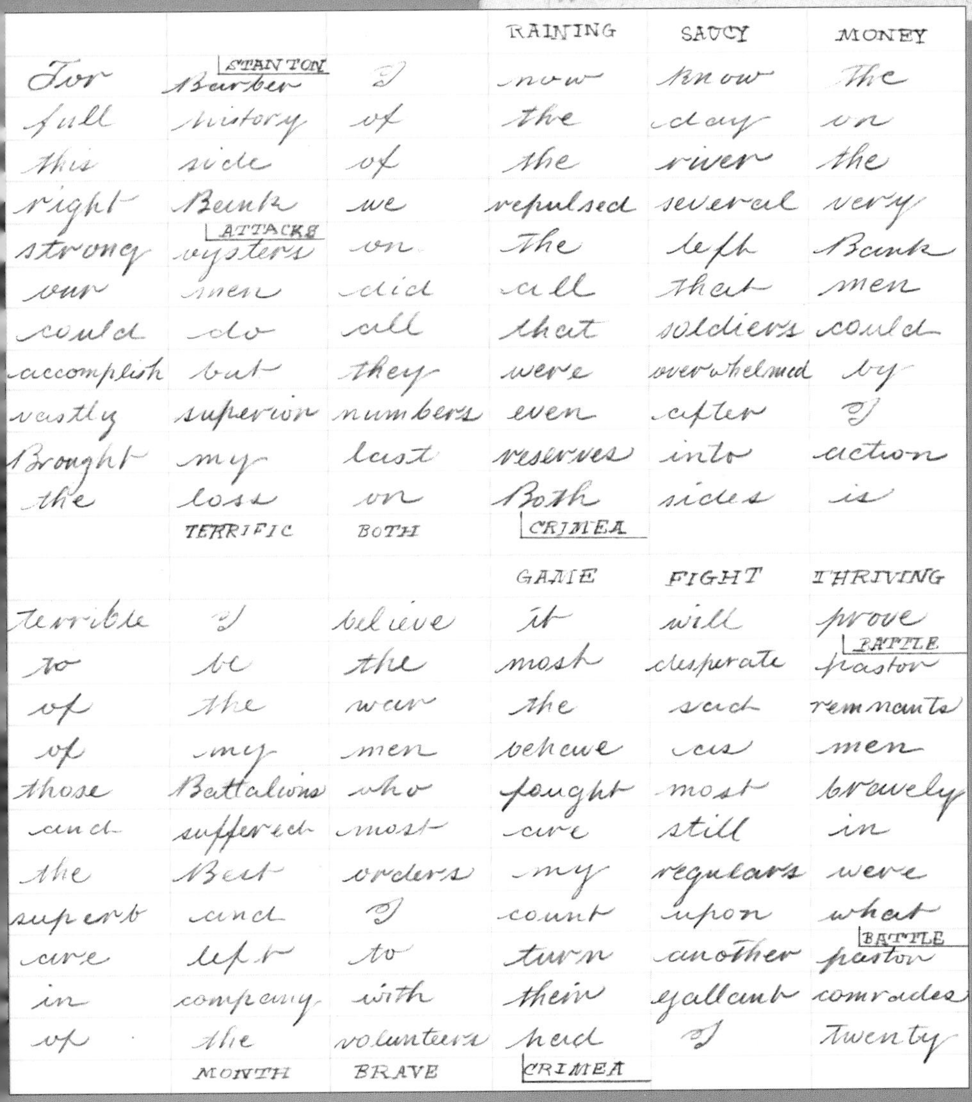

First block (column stop-words: STANTON, RAINING, SAUCY, MONEY at top; TERRIFIC, BOTH, CRIMEA at bottom):

	STANTON		RAINING	SAUCY	MONEY
For	Barber	I	now	know	The
full	history	of	the	day	on
this	side	of	the	river	the
right	Bank	we	repulsed	several	very
strong	oysters (ATTACKS)	on	The	left	Bank
our	men	did	all	that	men
could	do	all	that	soldiers	could
accomplish	but	they	were	overwhelmed	by
vastly	superior	numbers	even	after	I
Brought	my	last	reserves	into	action
the	loss	on	Both	sides	is
	TERRIFIC	BOTH	CRIMEA		

Second block (column stop-words: GAME, FIGHT, THRIVING at top; MONTH, BRAVE, CRIMEA at bottom):

			GAME	FIGHT	THRIVING
Terrible	I	believe	it	will	prove
to	be	the	most	desperate	raston (BATTLE)
of	the	war	the	sad	remnants
of	my	men	behave	is	men
those	Battalions	who	fought	most	bravely
and	suffered	most	are	still	in
the	Best	orders	my	regulars	were
superb	and	I	count	upon	what
are	left	to	turn	another	raston (BATTLE)
in	company	with	their	gallant	comrades
of	the	volunteers	had	I	Twenty
	MONTH	BRAVE	CRIMEA		

The General's Network

"Under the direction of General Grant, a large secret service force operated all over the Confederacy. It was probably the most effective secret service in the Federal army and General Grant came to rely on the information received from it."

COLONEL GEORGE E. SPENCER, U.S.A.

Ulysses S. Grant learned some lessons in the usefulness of spies early in the War. In September 1861 an agent employed by Grant's superior, General John C. Frémont, informed Grant that Confederate forces were preparing to advance on Paducah, Kentucky, a city strategically situated at the junction of the Ohio and Tennessee Rivers. Grant quickly moved to secure the town, and Paducah was occupied without a fight.

Seven months later, however, adequate intelligence was clearly lacking when nearly 40,000 Confederates were allowed to assemble and launch a surprise attack on Grant's lines at Shiloh Church in Tennessee.

So, in the autumn of 1862, as Major General Grant prepared to start the campaign that would eventually take him to Vicksburg, he determined that he would never again get caught short of information about the enemy. Grant, then commander of the Army of the Tennessee, resolved to build an espionage apparatus of his own, and to assign highly disciplined military men to run its farflung networks. As the War continued, Grant's organization would produce some remarkable performers: the superintendent of a key Southern railroad; an Alabama-born double agent who at various times spied for six generals — of whom four belonged to the enemy — and a Richmond spinster whose cover was her reputation as "Crazy Bet."

As in all military matters, Grant went to considerable pains in choosing a man to head

his nascent espionage apparatus in 1862. In casting about for candidates, he enlisted the help of his assistant adjutant general and close adviser, John A. Rawlins. The major recommended an officer he personally had never met; but Rawlins knew well of the man's reputation and thought him eminently qualified to become Grant's spymaster.

Brigadier General Grenville M. Dodge was born in Massachusetts and educated (with a degree in military and civil engineering) in Vermont and New Hampshire. As a young man he was infected by the railroad fever then sweeping the nation and headed west. Steeped in the dream that tracks would one day span the continent, Dodge worked as a surveyor for the Mississippi & Missouri Railroad, earning from Indians the nickname of Level Eye.

When the Civil War began, Dodge, aged 30, was mustered into service as a colonel, in command of the 4th Iowa Infantry. He was soon assigned to outpost duty at Rolla, Missouri, under General Frémont. Before long, Dodge found himself being pestered by orders requiring him to chase after phantom enemy forces that were conjured by Frémont's jittery imagination.

One day, after Dodge had returned from another futile expedition, he was approached by a Captain White, who commanded an independent company of Missouri Unionists. "Colonel," said White, "what's the use of wearing out all your cavalry horses trying to

Don't come — They are looking for some one I don't know who. Mrs. wife says you are suspected and your servant — The prosecuting Attorney says evidence sufficient exists to hang W— which they expect to obtain but have not yet succeeded in getting hold of it. Pole is feeling more and more uncomfortable —

Scrawled on a scrap of onionskin, a message smuggled out of Richmond by Union spy Elizabeth Van Lew warns one of her contacts to avoid the Confederate capital, where Miss Van Lew and her informers lived in constant fear of exposure. Many such dispatches were carried from the Van Lew mansion by a servant, who hid the scraps in the sole of his shoe.

run down rumors? I've got men in my company who know this section by heart, and I can get reliable information."

Dodge readily accepted and quickly organized the 1st Tennessee Cavalry, a group of scouts — regular soldiers who performed many of the functions of spies — to operate west of the Mississippi with White as their commander. And the scouting activities soon generated a network of civilian informants — Unionists living in Confederate-held territory. Using women to pass through picket lines on the pretext of visiting relatives, the Union sympathizers were able to smuggle out reports about the Confederates.

A significant payoff for Dodge's efforts came in March 1862. By then, Frémont was gone from the Western Theater, and Dodge's command had joined Brigadier General Samuel Curtis' army, which had recently pushed a large Confederate force southward out of Missouri and into Arkansas. Now the Confederates — 17,000 of them under Major General Earl Van Dorn — were on the move again, marching north, preparing for a clash at Pea Ridge, Arkansas. There Van Dorn planned to launch a surprise attack and then a double envelopment, and he very nearly brought it off. However, according to Dodge, just in the nick of time one of his scouts came riding in with "the news that Van Dorn's army was right on top of us, and this saved us."

At Pea Ridge Dodge had three horses shot from beneath him, suffered a hand wound and earned a promotion to brigadier general. After a month's leave of absence, he was transferred to western Tennessee, where his Missouri experience with scouts and spies was repeated. Hardly had he settled into his headquarters than in rode a regiment-size collection of mountain men, headed by a "Colonel" Hurst, who was incongruously attired in a tall silk hat and a long coat with brass buttons. To Hurst's demands that he and his men be sworn into regular service, Dodge readily agreed — correctly sensing that they would make fine scouts.

And just as had happened in Missouri, Dodge was able to develop an indigenous espionage network. Comprising the new scouts' kinfolk, it extended throughout the mountain country of western Tennessee.

In time, word of Dodge's skill in organizing irregulars reached John Rawlins and when the quest for an espionage chief began, it was small wonder that Rawlins advanced Dodge's name. Thus it happened that General Grant, on a day in October 1862, summoned Dodge to his headquarters in Jackson, Tennessee, and placed him in command of a division based in that district. Then Grant gave Dodge his most important assignment — to set up a spy ring that would "get only the facts" about the enemy.

In time, Dodge's network would number 117 field agents operating from Memphis to Mobile and from Atlanta to Richmond. Dodge paid his agents according to the danger and difficulty of the missions they undertook. One spy, for example, received $300 for keeping track of Confederate troop movements between Chattanooga and Murfreesboro, Tennessee; another got $750 for services rendered while living in Meridian and Jackson, Mississippi. Moreover, before a spy set out on a long assignment, he (or she) was given from $5,000 to $10,000 — in Confederate money — to defray expenses.

Historically, government bursars have seldom been generous with espionage operations, and the Civil War was no exception. To cope with chronic fund shortages, Dodge — with Grant's consent — hit upon the expedient of using money derived from the sale of confiscated Southern cotton. Such transactions were clearly illegal, and bureaucratic protests were eventually carried to Grant. The commanding general turned a deaf ear, and Grenville Dodge continued to finance his network with cotton money.

During the War and after, Dodge fiercely protected the identity of his agents. He alone knew their names; even his own staff officers were given only the number that had been assigned to each spy. Once, Dodge's determination to safeguard the security of his people brought him into direct conflict with a military superior, Major General Stephen A. Hurlbut, then commanding the Union XVI Corps in Memphis. Hurlbut demanded to know the names of spies who were operating in his jurisdiction. Dodge not only turned him down flat but, when Hurlbut insisted, appealed to Grant for support. As he nearly always did, Grant upheld Dodge.

As a professional engineer and surveyor, Grenville Dodge had a lifelong interest in geography and topography, and in his headquarters he kept large maps of the South, which he continually filled in with data received from his spies and scouts. Thus, in an exercise useful both to Grant and to Dodge himself in his capacity as commander of a

combat division, even the briefest mention in an agent's report of a creek or woodland or hill would soon be translated into a notation on one of Dodge's maps.

For Dodge's network, Grant's Vicksburg Campaign of 1863 offered a major test — and the spies rose to the occasion, giving information that was vital to Grant in his maneu-

Brigadier General Grenville Dodge combined management of the Federal spy service in the west with the command of a combat division. Guided by his spies' reports on a raid into northern Alabama in 1863, Dodge and his division took 1,000 horses and mules, destroyed 1.5 million bushels of corn, burned five cotton mills and tore up 30 miles of railroad track.

vering and in his subsequent siege of the city.

Although the Confederates had assiduously spread the word that General Joseph Johnston possessed 60,000 troops with which to assail Grant's rear, Dodge's agents correctly reported that Johnston had fewer than 30,000 — a number Grant felt certain he could handle. Later, a spy named Sanborn accurately informed Dodge of the forces available to the Confederates as they made a stand at Champion's Hill outside Vicksburg; the information proved critical to the Union victory — one that sent Confederate General John C. Pemberton's army reeling back to Vicksburg's defenses. During the ensuing siege, one of Dodge's agents, Jane Featherstone, kept an eye on another Confederate force as it camped 50 miles to the east, while an illiterate girl named Mary Malone reported on farflung enemy dispositions in Mississippi and Alabama.

And then there was Philip Henson, described by Dodge as "probably the ablest man in our secret service."

Henson possessed many attributes that made him ideal spy material. He was a native Southerner and had no need to fake the accents of the region. As a lifelong wanderer, he knew the territory as few others did. As a naturally amiable sort, always generous with offerings from the supply of "good old rye" that he carried wherever he went, Henson had a way of ingratiating himself with people low and high. And above all else, he hated secession and loved the Union.

Born in northeast Alabama, Henson went to school for a brief time and then, as one of seven children whose father had died when Philip was 12, he stepped out on his own. Forever footloose, Henson drove cattle, car-

ried mail, and traveled to Kansas and to New Mexico. He finally returned to roam through Alabama, Georgia and Mississippi, all the while making friends who would later stand him in good stead.

By the start of the Civil War, Henson was married and working in a Mississippi country store. Having no wish whatever to soldier for the Confederacy, he persuaded the owner of a nearby cotton plantation to hire him as overseer — a job that carried with it an exemption from military service. In late 1862, as Grant thrust into Mississippi, overrunning the region where he lived, Henson took an oath of loyalty to the Union not, as many of his neighbors did, out of coercion but because, he said, "I believed in it."

Henson did more than swear loyalty; he agreed to spy for the Union's Major General William S. Rosecrans — an arrangement that soon led to Henson's being hauled as a prisoner before the man who would soon become his steadiest employer and greatest admirer.

Henson was arrested in November 1862 when he was returning from one of his first assignments, a foray aimed at ascertaining the plans of the Confederacy's General Braxton Bragg. On his way through the lines, Henson was stopped by Union pickets wary of deep-drawling Southerners no matter what sort of papers they carried.

Demanding that he be taken to the nearest headquarters, Henson soon found himself confronted by none other than Grenville Dodge. Soon persuaded as to the true nature of Henson's mission, and impressed by the information that he had gathered, Dodge enlisted the Alabamian as a spy for himself rather than Rosecrans.

At the time, Vicksburg was uppermost in the minds of Ulysses S. Grant and his gener-

IN THE ENEMY'S WORKS.

BOOTY.

IN PURSUIT.

These engravings by Thomas Nast trace the career of an imaginary Federal spy, including the theft of war plans from a Confederate officers' tent (*left center*) and their delivery to Union officers (*right center*). The circular panels depict the fate of an unlucky spy: capture and execution.

als. Assigned to report on the town's defenses, Henson put to work the techniques that would characterize all his operations behind enemy lines.

From his prewar acquaintances in northern Mississippi, Henson selected a fire-snorting secessionist named Jesse Johnsey to be his unwitting accomplice. With an extra horse in tow, Henson rode up to Johnsey's house one day and suggested that the two go to Vicksburg, where several of Johnsey's seven sons were serving in the Confederate Army. And so, with scarcely a hitch, they went on their way, easing past Confederate pickets with offerings from Henson's bottle and his simple explanation that he and Jesse were "going to see our boys in Vicksburg."

Once in the city, Henson gained the assistance of a Confederate captain who spoke favorably of him to General Pemberton. Given the run of the city and its defenses by Pemberton, the spy took mental notes of everything that he saw or heard and filed them away in his remarkable memory. When Henson finally made his way back to Union lines and divulged what he had learned, Dodge was so pleased that he gave the spy a fine horse named Black Hawk.

Dodge also provided Henson with a modus operandi. Dodge had a pet theory that his agents should have something to offer the Confederates they encountered on their journeys. To that end, Dodge frequently provided his spies with seemingly important but actually harmless pieces of military information that they could use to insinuate themselves into the confidence of enemy officers.

Thus, on one occasion, Dodge trustingly told Henson, "Go to my desk and take whatever you think will help you most with the rebs." Selecting several schedules for Union

SUSPECTED.

WHO GOES THERE.

THE

LIFE

OF A

SPY.

SAFE RETURN.

SENTENCE.

TELLING HIS ADVENTURES.

Th. Nast.

military projects, Henson embarked on an expedition behind Union lines that eventually took him to the Georgia headquarters of Lieutenant General Leonidas Polk, one of the Confederacy's foremost commanders. Henson introduced himself and forthrightly explained that he had come to offer information taken from a Federal headquarters. Polk was so impressed by what Henson knew about Federal activities that he put the Union spy on his own espionage payroll with a starting stipend of $500.

Similarly, at other times during his service Henson was employed as a double agent by at least three Confederate generals — David Ruggles, Samuel Gholson and Samuel Ferguson. And so, armed on the one hand with passes from various Confederate commanders and, on the other, with one from the Union's Dodge (which he kept hidden in a hollow beneath the brass plate on the butt of his pistol), Philip Henson repeatedly made his way between hostile camps — until May 1864, when Dodge dispatched his prize agent on what he promised would be Henson's final mission. And so it was.

Sent to spy on the activities of the Confederacy's ferocious cavalryman, Nathan Bedford Forrest, Henson was arrested in Tupelo, Mississippi, by some of Forrest's men. The cavalry leader had heard of Henson's peregrinations across the lines — and suspected him of treason. Unlike other Southern generals, Forrest was immune to Henson's persuasions — if only because he ignored Henson's requests for an audience.

For months, Henson languished in solitary cells, being transferred from one prison to another. During one period he was confined in a tiny, windowless room known as "the sweat box." Yet somehow he survived, and in February 1865, Confederate authorities, in their desperation for men to bear arms, agreed to Henson's request that he be permitted to serve in "the old bloody 26th Mississippi" with General Robert E. Lee's army in Virginia.

What happened next is unclear, although Dodge later hinted that his network had bribed Confederate guards to let Henson escape. At any rate, while in transit to Virginia, Henson jumped off a train and, in the War's final days, somehow reached safety behind the Union lines.

Later, when he learned of Henson's exploits, Nathan Bedford Forrest, regretting only that he had not hanged the agent when he had him, paid Henson a left-handed tribute. Philip Henson, said Forrest, had been "the most dangerous Federal spy operating in the Confederacy."

For the most part, General Dodge devoted his energies to commanding his division and to directing large-scale intelligence operations for the Union's western army; he left local counterespionage to his subordinates. But on one occasion Dodge almost inadvertently became involved in spycatching — and he would rue it for the rest of his life.

In November 1863 Grant's forces lay besieged in Chattanooga, with the Confederates of General Bragg glowering down on them from Lookout Mountain. Bragg suspected that Grant would soon receive reinforcements, and it was critical that the Confederate commander find out the strength and disposition of the fresh Federal forces. To that end, Bragg dispatched a band of scouts into the countryside. Among them were the members of a group that had become notorious to Federal authorities as

A stained-glass window commissioned by the Tennessee Division of the United Daughters of the Confederacy memorializes Sam Davis, the "boy hero," who chose death rather than betray his leader. The window hangs in the Museum of the Confederacy in Richmond, Virginia.

Coleman's Scouts. In fact, the band was led by a Captain Henry Shaw, who went under the pseudonym of E. C. Coleman.

On November 19 two of Dodge's agents, both dressed in Confederate uniforms, chanced upon a young man riding along a road about 15 miles south of Pulaski, Tennessee, where Dodge was headquartered. To explain their own presence, the scouts pretended that they were rounding up men to serve in the Confederate Army. When the pair threatened to conscript the lone rider, he panicked, insisting that he was on urgent business for General Bragg and displaying a pass signed by "E. Coleman" — the man for whom every Federal in the area was looking.

That was more than enough. Taken at gunpoint to Dodge's headquarters, the prisoner turned out to be 21-year-old Sam Davis of Smyrna, Tennessee, who was later described by Dodge as "a fine, soldierly looking young fellow." Sewn into his saddle and in his cavalry boots was a rich bounty of incriminating material that Davis, during a recent rendezvous with Captain Shaw, had received for delivery to Bragg.

One message, for example, would have informed Bragg that "the Yankees are still camped on the line of the L & ARR. Genl Dodges Hd Qrs are at Pulaski. His main force is camped from that place to Lynnville. Some at Elk river & 2 Regts at Athens." Highly embarrassing to Dodge was a penciled draft of his own monthly report; the document had obviously been filched from his desk, most likely by a former slave named Houston, who had attached himself as a servant to Dodge's headquarters.

Aware from the pass that Davis was a member of the Coleman Scouts, Grenville Dodge himself undertook the ensuing interrogations, repeatedly offering young Davis not only his life but his freedom in return for information about his leader. Time after time, Sam Davis refused — despite the fact that he knew that Captain Henry Shaw, or E. Coleman himself, was even then a prisoner in the same jail in which Davis was being held.

In an incident entirely unrelated to Davis' capture, Shaw had been taken prisoner by Federal scouts who had come across "an old, seedy, awkward-looking man in citizen's clothes" who described himself as a former Confederate surgeon. Shaw was brought to the jail in Pulaski, where he saw Sam Davis and knew that Davis had recognized him. For seven days, Shaw endured an agony of suspense lest Davis break down under questioning and reveal his identity.

He need not have worried: Sam Davis had already chosen another course.

By now Grenville Dodge was virtually pleading with the youngster, whom he had grown to like and whose courage he would forever admire. But it was no use. Davis remained silent, and given the evidence against the youth, Dodge had little choice but to turn him over to a court-martial board. The board convened on November 24, found Davis guilty and sentenced him to be hanged on November 27, the day after Thanksgiving. Still, Dodge repeatedly offered to commute the sentence, and Davis refused to cooperate. On the eve of his execution, Sam Davis wrote a final letter to his mother. "I have got to die tomorrow morning," he began matter-of-factly. "Mother, I do not hate to die."

The next morning Davis mounted the scaffold, and again an offer was made to spare his life. As a witness later wrote, Davis replied that to answer Dodge would be to betray a friend. "And he absolute-ly Refused to Purchase his life by sacrifising that of his Friend."

A sack was put over Davis' head, and the trap dropped.

Henry Shaw would survive the War, albeit under a cloud as the man who lived because Davis died. As for Grenville Dodge, he was severely wounded leading troops during the 1864 campaign for Atlanta; after he recovered, he was placed in command of the Department of Missouri. Many years later, when in his seventies, Dodge would reach into an old man's fading memory and be moved to contribute $10 toward a monument then being built in Nashville to honor the Southern martyr, Sam Davis.

In March 1864 Grant moved East to become General in Chief of all the Union armies and set up headquarters in the field with the Army of the Potomac. He inherited as his espionage chief an officer of contradictory character. It would appear that George H. Sharpe, an erstwhile New York lawyer, hid behind a roistering exterior a keen knack for the cold, silent business of espionage.

Sharpe originally was chosen for his job by Major General Joseph Hooker for reasons that may have been more social than military. On assuming command of the Army of the Potomac soon after the Battle of Fredericksburg, Hooker set up a headquarters that quickly became notorious for its dissolute ways. One officer said that Hooker's tent was a place where "no gentleman cared to go and to which no lady could go." General George Meade simply wrote of Hooker: "I do not like his entourage."

Colonel George H. Sharpe, appointed head of the Army of the Potomac's Bureau of Military Information in March of 1863, seemed to some too convivial a man for so sensitive a position: That same month his superior, General Marsena Patrick, spotted Sharpe and a fellow officer stumbling back to their quarters "as tight as bricks." Nevertheless, Sharpe and his scouts soon were supplying the army command with highly accurate information.

One of the most conspicuous members of that entourage was Major General Dan Sickles, a onetime Tammany Hall politician whose scandalous private affairs had at various times attracted national attention. Sickles was accompanied to some of Hooker's revelries by a subordinate officer with similarly bibulous inclinations. Colonel George Sharpe, a handsome, mustachioed man, appreciated a good time at least as much as his immediate superior. Indeed, Sickles himself would one day note that Sharpe was "quite too fond of a nice time, loves fun and is very irregular in all his ways."

That, at any rate, may explain how Sharpe, the little-known commander of a regiment from upstate New York, caught Hooker's eye. What is certain is that Hooker created a Bureau of Military Information for the Army of the Potomac and reached far down in the ranks to make Sharpe its chief.

Ostensibly, Sharpe's operation came under the aegis of Brigadier General Marsena R. Patrick, imperious provost marshal general of the Army of the Potomac. From Patrick's diary, however, it is clear that he was at best barely aware of the details of Sharpe's espionage activities — and that he resented the fact. Once, he complained that he had had to speak to Sharpe "very unpleasantly, for meddling with matters that do not belong at all to him." Again, Patrick approvingly noted a fellow officer's opinion that Sharpe was "Tricky and full of all sorts of Policy" — which, if Patrick had thought about it, were not bad traits for a spy chief to possess.

The first major test for Sharpe's Bureau of Military Information was Hooker's Chancellorsville Campaign, and Sharpe's estimates of enemy strength were within an extraordinary .25 of 1 percent of pinpoint accuracy.

Yet in the bitterness of his Chancellorsville defeat, Hooker cast blame on everyone but himself. He criticized the Bureau of Military Information so roundly that even Marsena Patrick was moved to defend it. Hooker, Patrick wrote, "has treated our 'Secret Service Department,' which has furnished him with the most astonishingly correct information, with insult."

Later, during the Gettysburg Campaign, one of Sharpe's scouts, a dashing young captain named John C. Babcock, kept Lee's army under continual observation, trailing it as it advanced to the Potomac, crossed the river and moved into Pennsylvania. Yet in the aftermath of the Battle of Gettysburg, Hooker's successor, George Meade, scorned for his timidity in pursuing the defeated Confederates, also turned against the secret service. He threatened to fire Sharpe and disband the Bureau of Military Information.

Ulysses S. Grant put a stop to all that. Grant obviously sensed that in George Sharpe he had a spymaster who would meet his exacting standards.

On one occasion, however, Sharpe ventured briefly into counterespionage, and in that endeavor he was less than successful. Caught short by time, he was unable to prevent a calamity that might well have cost General Grant his life.

The incident occurred shortly before noon on August 9, 1864, at City Point, Virginia, where Grant had established his headquarters and supply base on the south side of the James River near Petersburg. Grant, sitting in front of his tent, had just been informed by Sharpe of the suspected presence of Confederate spies. After assuring Grant that he had a plan to nab the agents, Sharpe departed. And at that moment, in the words of one

of Grant's aides, "a terrific explosion shook the earth." Recalled another: "Such a rain of shot, shell, bullets, pieces of wood, iron bars and bolts, chains and missiles of every kind was never before witnessed. It was terrible — awful — terrific."

One of Grant's orderlies was killed and three men in his immediate vicinity were wounded. Throughout, with the deadly debris falling around him, Grant sat without batting an eye.

In all, 58 were killed and 126 injured in the explosion of ammunition stores at City Point — which had been the work of one John Maxwell, a captain in the Confederate secret service. Maxwell had fashioned a bomb of 12 pounds of powder and a timing device and had put it in an innocent-looking wooden candle box. Wearing a passable disguise, he had coolly made his way through the milling throng of City Point soldiers and laborers down to a wharf laden with ammunition. There, Maxwell had talked his way aboard an ammunition barge and handed his bomb to a worker, explaining that the barge's captain wished it stored below. By the time of the explosion, Maxwell was safely out of harm's way.

Although the disaster was attributed by the Federals to workmen's carelessness in handling ammunition, one of Grant's staff officers later recalled that "there was suspicion in the minds of many of us that it was the work of some emissaries of the enemy." However, no official blame fell on Sharpe. And it was during Sharpe's collaboration with Grant that the efforts of two of the North's most valuable spies came into fullest flower.

Late in 1862, Robert E. Lee's Army of Northern Virginia was stretched along the

In the sketch at left, an explosion rips through the massive Federal munitions depot along the James River at City Point, Virginia, on August 9, 1864. The blast, which was the work of a Confederate secret agent, occurred under the noses of General Grant and his spymaster, George Sharpe. A few minutes later, Grant telegraphed Washington, reporting several casualties near his headquarters tent and adding that "damage at the wharf must be considerable," an assessment borne out by the photograph below.

south bank of the Rappahannock River near Fredericksburg; deployed on the opposite bank was the Army of the Potomac, then under Major General Ambrose Burnside. Although Lee was ideally situated to block any direct enemy move toward Richmond, he was worried that a precarious supply situation might force him to retreat. The focus of Lee's concern was the performance of the Richmond, Fredericksburg & Potomac Railroad, whose single track along the 55-mile stretch from Richmond to Hamilton's Crossing near Fredericksburg was his only line of supply by rail. On December 8 Lee wrote to President Davis: "Unless the Richmond and Fredericksburg Railroad is more energetically operated, it will be impossible to supply this army with provisions, and oblige its retirement to Hanover Station."

Five days later, Burnside's disastrous assault against the hills behind Fredericksburg saved Lee the necessity of retreat. Yet in January, with the opposing armies still facing each other across the Rappahannock, Lee remained fretful. Again he wrote to Davis, this time complaining about the lack of "energy and zeal" on the part of RF & P officials —

and going so far as to urge that the railroad's superintendent be replaced.

The superintendent in question was Samuel Ruth. There is no solid evidence that he was deliberately impeding the operations of the RF & P at that time, but it is a fact that by 1864 Ruth was very active indeed as a Union spy in the service of Colonel George Sharpe.

Little is known about Ruth's background or personality save that he was born in Pennsylvania, worked as a mechanic, moved to Virginia in 1839, and was at one point described by a Richmond newspaper as "a most efficient railroad officer, and a respectable, prudent and cautious man with a most marked disposition to mind only his own business." As for his methods of espionage, it is apparent only that Ruth had a collaborator, one Frederick W. E. Lohman, and that Ruth communicated with Federal authorities through a courier, a Virginian named Charles Carter, whom Sharpe provided.

Perhaps inevitably, Ruth furnished to Sharpe information pertaining almost exclusively to Confederate supplies and troop movements — the sort of information that required no cloak-and-dagger work but would come to a railroad executive in the course of an ordinary day's work. Thus, Ruth reported on damage to track and rolling stock in the Richmond-Petersburg area, on the strength of Confederate guards along the RF & P and Virginia Central Railroads, on the amount of supplies transferred to railroads from the ships of blockade runners and on the commissary stores carried by the RF & P. Ruth also alerted Sharpe about Confederate dispositions in southwestern Virginia just before a Union cavalry raid through that area in December 1864 and, in that same month, on the number of troops detached by rail to meet a Union expedition against Wilmington, North Carolina.

But some of Ruth's endeavors on behalf of the Union extended beyond the collecting of information to another form of irregular activity — which very nearly did him in. As part of a well-organized underground, Ruth helped fugitive Federal prisoners of war, Southern dissidents and Confederate Army deserters in their northward flight. Early in 1865, some of those fugitives were intercepted in East Richmond and interrogated, after which Ruth's collaborator, Lohman, was arrested. And on January 23 Samuel Ruth was taken into custody at his office in the Richmond depot of the RF & P and then jailed in Castle Thunder.

His imprisonment lasted for only nine days. At a hearing held on February 1, Ruth somehow convinced a Confederate commissioner that his accusers were persons to whom he had refused free railroad rides. After the commissioner found that there was not "a particle of evidence" against him, Ruth stepped forth a free man — and something of a hero. "It is outrageous," cried the Richmond *Whig*, "that a respectable citizen should be seized and thrown into the abominable hole, Castle Thunder, upon no better ground than a malicious whisper."

No sooner was he freed than Ruth returned to being a railroader — and a spy. Indeed, less than a month after his release — and only a few weeks before the end of the War — Ruth scored what was probably his greatest espionage coup. In so doing, he wrought the destruction of his own railroad.

Sometime late in February, a Confederate quartermaster officer called on Ruth and asked for his cooperation in transporting to Hamilton's Crossing 400,000 pounds of Southern tobacco that was to be exchanged for 95 tons of bacon, valued at $380,000, that was being smuggled out of the North. Ruth informed one of George Sharpe's couriers, and on March 5 General Grant ordered a raid on the RF & P depot near Fredericksburg. Not only was the Confederate tobacco seized, but 400 prisoners were taken, the depot was burned and 28 freight cars were destroyed — along with four principal railroad bridges south of Fredericksburg.

After the War, Brevet Major General Sharpe, supporting the compensatory claims of Ruth and two other agents, paid them a high compliment. He wrote that in estimating the value of their espionage services he was "unwilling to name a less sum than forty thousand dollars."

Another who chimed in with a letter on Ruth's behalf was a gentlewoman from one of Richmond's best families. Her name was Elizabeth Van Lew, and she was herself a perfect example of the untrained Civil War spy who, overcoming a background incongruous to her new calling, made up for her inexperience with ingenuity.

Elizabeth Van Lew, a tiny, birdlike creature with a sharp, peckish nose, bright, blue eyes and hair done in ringlets, was a charitable soul; and her beneficence in Richmond took the form of frequent visits to Libby Prison with baskets of goodies for "her boys."

Her boys were the Federal prisoners who populated the infamous prison. Those prisoners, especially the more recent arrivals, were filled with valuable information about the strength and dispositions of Confederate troops they had seen while being sent from the fighting fronts to prison in Richmond.

Little is known about the specific informa-

Elizabeth Van Lew, the Union spy living in Richmond, so charmed the city's provost marshal, John Winder, that he allowed her charitable visits to Federal prisoners of war, who then supplied her with intelligence. "I can flatter almost anything out of old Winder," she wrote, "his personal vanity is so great."

tion contained in Elizabeth Van Lew's reports to Sharpe and other Union officers: Several years after her death, efforts to examine her War Department dossier drew only a response that "all papers in this department relating to Miss Van Lew were taken from the files on December 12, 1866, and given to her." There the trail ends. However, many of the details of how Van Lew obtained that information and passed it on to Union authorities are contained in her long, rambling diary. Found buried outside her mansion, it went beyond her wartime activities to cover her entire life in Richmond, the city she loved — but whose values she loathed.

Of colonial stock, she was the daughter of a prosperous and respected hardware merchant who had built an elegant three-and-a-half-story mansion atop Church Hill, the highest of Richmond's seven hills. During Elizabeth's girlhood, Chief Justice John Marshall was a frequent visitor to the Van Lew home, and the famous Swedish soprano, Jenny Lind, later sang in its parlor.

Sent to a Philadelphia school, Elizabeth returned a dedicated abolitionist. "Slave power," she wrote in her diary, "is arrogant, is jealous and intrusive, is cruel, is despotic." Exercising her beliefs, Elizabeth soon persuaded her widowed mother to free the nine slaves owned by the family. Then, as war approached, she wrote that she became "a silent and sorrowing spectator of the rise and spread of the secession mania."

On April 17, 1861, five days after Fort Sumter was bombarded, Elizabeth Van Lew first saw the Confederate banner flying over Richmond. Then, after witnessing a torchlight parade one night, she fell to her knees overcome by a revelation of duty. "Never," she wrote later, "did a feeling of more calm determination and high resolve for endurance come over me."

She soon found a way to exercise her resolution. At the foot of Church Hill and within view of the Van Lew garden lay the ship chandler's warehouse that had been converted to Libby Prison. Having heard of the suffering that Union captives were enduring within its baleful confines, Elizabeth began carrying baskets of food, medicine and books to the prisoners.

To be sure, she became the target of what she described as "the threats, the scowls, the frowns of an infuriated community." But even embroiled in the passions of the Civil War, Richmond remained a civilized society, and no steps were taken to stop the Van Lew visitations. After all, what harm could possibly be done by a woman who had already become known as "Crazy Bet"?

Elizabeth Van Lew polished that image. Even before the War she had been considered strange, if only because of her outspoken abolitionist sentiments. Now she emphasized her eccentricities — mumbling to herself as she walked the streets, often assuming a vacant expression, allowing the ringlets of her hair to fall into disarray and wearing her shabbiest clothes.

Behind that façade was a shrewd and resourceful mind that improvised as it worked. In her original naïveté, Van Lew simply wrote down her gleanings from Union prisoners and posted them as letters to Federal authorities; incredibly, some of the letters arrived at their intended destinations.

Gradually the Van Lew operation became more sophisticated. In the books their benefactress had loaned them, the prisoners faintly underlined certain words that constituted an impromptu code for her. Van Lew devised her own cipher — after her death, it was found folded in the back of her watch, where she had carried it for nearly 40 years. Using her household servants as couriers — several of the Van Lew slaves had stayed on after being given their freedom — Elizabeth sent them northward carrying baskets filled with farm produce. Each basket held some eggs, one of which had been emptied of its natural contents and now contained a tiny slip of paper bearing an enciphered message.

The Federal prisoners were by no means Van Lew's only sources of information. She was a good listener, and Libby's Confederate guards often were careless in their talk. She also went out of her way to cultivate the prison's commandant, Lieutenant David H. Todd (whose half sister was Mrs. Abraham Lincoln), by plying him with buttermilk and gingerbread while engaging him in pleasant — and informative — conversation. Later, when Todd was assigned to other duty, Elizabeth actually inveigled his successor, a Lieutenant Gibbs, to move into the Van Lew mansion with his family as boarders.

Slowly the circle of sources widened. As a Union officer said after the War, Elizabeth Van Lew and her mother, who had gradually joined in the espionage enterprise, "had clerks in the rebel war and navy departments in their confidence." Moreover, in what was doubtless a most satisfying success, the spinster-spy actually penetrated the Confederate President's house.

Several years before the War, Elizabeth had at her own expense sent one of her freed slaves, a highly intelligent girl named Mary Elizabeth Bowser, North to be educated. Now the young woman was summoned, and after some coaching from her former owner, she found employment on the household

staff of Jefferson Davis. As a dining-room servant, she was privy to the mealtime conversations of the Confederacy's President.

As the War progressed, the Union high command recognized the value of Van Lew's contributions. During the early part of the conflict, she had communicated with the Union's Major General Ben Butler, then in command at Fort Monroe on the Peninsula, who referred to her as "my correspondent in Richmond." After serving in the Western Theater, Butler returned to Virginia in 1864 and managed to get his forces bottled up at Bermuda Hundred near Richmond. He again began hearing from Elizabeth Van Lew — although more sporadically. By now, she had been taken under more powerful wings. As she explained, when "the war advanced and the army closed around Richmond, I was able to communicate with General Butler and General Grant, but not so well and persistently with General Butler, for there was too much danger in the system and persons. With General Grant, through

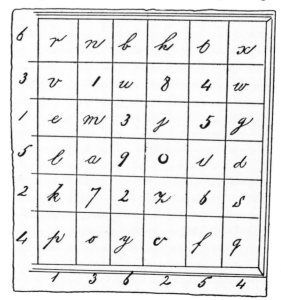

As her espionage activities grew more sophisticated, Elizabeth Van Lew developed a communications cipher based on the key at left, which was discovered folded in her watchcase after her death. The 36-box grid contains the letters of the alphabet and the numbers zero through nine, each of which would be represented in ciphered messages by its coordinates: For example, the letter *e* could be encoded as 11, the number 7 as 23.

his Chief of Secret Service, General George H. Sharpe, I was more fortunate."

By the end of the War, Van Lew had established five relay stations for her courier system. According to Sharpe, General Grant repeatedly demanded "specific information," and she "steadily conveyed it to him." So speedily did her system work that, in addition to the military information she transmitted, she was able to provide Grant's table with flowers still fresh from her garden.

At long last, the way was cleared for Grant's army to enter Richmond, and Elizabeth Van Lew with her own hands raised atop her mansion the first Union flag to fly over Richmond in four years. Just before the arrival of the first Union troops, angry citizens of Richmond threatened violence, but the little spinster, her ringlets bobbing angrily, faced them down. "I know you, and you, and you," she cried, pointing to individuals and calling them by name. "General Grant will be in this city within the hour; if this house is harmed, your houses shall be burned by noon." The mob melted away.

When Grant entered Richmond, one of his first acts was to visit the Van Lew home to take tea on the columned porch with his highly regarded spy. And later, Grant put his gratitude on paper, writing to her: "You have sent me the most valuable information received from Richmond during the war."

After the War, the Union's spymasters flourished. Allan Pinkerton expanded his successful Chicago detective agency, establishing branches in Philadelphia and New York. Grenville Dodge, appointed chief engineer of the Union Pacific Railroad in its thrust across the continent, placed his mark upon the face and future of America. George H. Sharpe received a job as Surveyor for the Port of New York, and was prominent in the politics of his native state.

In direct contrast, the spies who had worked in the field were shabbily treated by the Union for which they had imperiled their lives and livelihoods. Despite Sharpe's plea on behalf of Samuel Ruth, that spy received a measly $500; after Ruth's death in 1872, a committee of the U.S. House of Representatives, deciding upon a request by his widow for financial relief, ruled that her petition "should not be granted."

Similarly, Dodge's stellar spy, Philip Henson, was refused reward for his services. To eke out a living, he took to the lecture trail. And to promote his tours, he appeared on the podium with a six-foot-three-inch-long beard that he claimed was "the longest beard of any living man." As he wrote to Dodge, since "Congress has refused to allow me anything for my services during the war, I have decided to adopt this method to help keep myself and wife in our old age."

Elizabeth Van Lew continued to live in the mansion on Church Hill, reviled by the citizens of Richmond. "No one will walk with us on the street," she wrote, "no one will go with us anywhere; and it grows worse and worse as the years roll on." She died in 1900 in abject poverty. A monument was placed on her grave, and the inscription read:

She risked everything that is dear to man — friends, fortune, comfort, health, life itself, all for the one absorbing desire of her heart — that slavery might be abolished and the Union preserved.

It was erected by admirers from Boston.

How to Wreck a Railroad

Confederate raiders behind Federal army lines proved particularly adept at tearing up railroad track, causing untold headaches for Union supply officers — and especially for Brigadier General Herman Haupt, field chief of the Federal military rail system.

Bent on retaliation, Haupt in 1863 produced one of the Civil War's more remarkable documents: a detailed instruction manual, illustrated with photographs, that taught Federal cavalrymen how to wreck trackage behind Confederate lines — quickly, thoroughly and scientifically. A number of the photographs from Haupt's manual, taken by A. J. Russell, appear here and on the following pages. In the pictures members of Haupt's trained railroad Construction Corps — mostly lured civilian railroad workers and former slaves — demonstrate the new wrecking techniques and then show how such damage could be repaired or even prevented.

Haupt's manual stressed speed; Union cavalry raiders on hit-and-run forays in hostile territory could not spend all day levering up track. Nor could they carry crowbars or other heavy implements. Haupt's solution: small iron wedges that could be pounded with axes between the rails and ties to pry loose the most stubborn spikes (*below*) and steel hooks to remove the rest. With these tools, Haupt boasted, "four men can remove a rail in three minutes."

Rendering rails unfit for use took only a bit of chain or an iron rod driven into the ground to serve as a fulcrum. Then, as Haupt described the experiment shown at right, "men carried the rail around, bending it at the place where it is spiked, and finally breaking it at that point."

Two of Haupt's men pry up a track by hammering in wedges while another employs a horse to bend a rail that has one end lashed down with a chain.

Having braced a loose rail against another one in place, a work team bends the loose rail around an iron rod that has been driven deeply between two ties.

In Haupt's experiment, workers made two piles of ties, then laid rails across each pile. Even adding coal oil failed to produce a blaze hot enough to warp the rails.

Building Bonfires to Warp Rails

Haupt scorned the Confederates' normal method of warping rails by laying them on top of piles of burning ties until they sagged of their own weight. The damage was easily undone, he maintained. "Rails which are simply bent can, with the use of levers and sledges, be straightened so as to permit their use."

Moreover, burning took too much time for Haupt. To be sure, if the fires burned long enough, Haupt admitted, the rails became so soft that they could be "bent around trees, forming sometimes complete circles." But during Haupt's own experiment *(left)*, three hours passed and still "the rails had not become heated to any considerable extent."

A Federal soldier surveys wreckage on the Orange & Alexandria. Enemy raiders have bent some rails, twisted others and pulled down telegraph wires.

A New Tool for Ripping, Twisting and Bending

To render rails permanently useless to the Confederacy's railroads, Haupt and an assistant, E. C. Smeed, came up with the ruthlessly effective steel hook shown below. Double-pronged and resembling an oversize horseshoe, the hook could be fitted with a handle — any strong pole would do — and inserted under one end of a length of track. When leverage was applied, the steel hook would rip the rail from the ties and twist it "spirally," said Haupt, "like a corkscrew or auger" — making repair nearly impossible.

Haupt was proud of the 6½-pound "portable contrivance," which he claimed was "the most expeditious mode yet devised of tearing up track."

A civilian railroad official (*left*) holds a pair of track-bending hooks while an officer points to a short length of thoroughly twisted track.

wing how to twist a rail, work-crew members *(left)* use a pole and hook to hold one end steady while others, using a pole as a lever, give the track a corkscrew bend.

A Haupt railroader bores a hole in a wooden support of a bridge probably near Haupt's Alexandria, Virginia, headquarters, where wrecking equipment was tes

A "Torpedo" for Blowing Up Bridges

"A simple and expeditious mode of destroying bridges," Haupt wrote in his formal engineer's prose, "is often a desideratum" when wrecking an enemy railroad.

Haupt's fertile mind came up with just the tool for the job: an eight-inch-long "torpedo" *(below)* made of metal cylinders filled with black powder. Equipped with a fuse, it was placed in a hole bored with an auger *(left)* in a bridge's main brace. On exploding, the torpedo destroyed the brace so effectively, Haupt wrote, that "two torpedoes will suffice to throw down" a simple truss bridge. More complex spans required two additional torpedoes, but even then Haupt declared that the entire destructive process required "a period of time not exceeding five minutes."

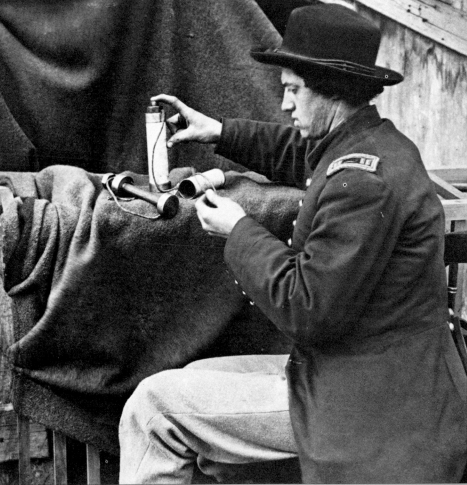

An officer assembles a bridge-destroying torpedo. In one test, Haupt said, a torpedo shattered a heavy timber, throwing pieces "more than 100 feet."

A Federal locomotive derailed by Confederate raiders lies on its side by the Orange & Alexandria tracks near Brandy Station, Virginia, in 1864. Derailed eng

uld be righted and repaired. A more effective method of rendering them "unfit for service," related Haupt, was "to fire a cannon ball through the boiler."

A repair crew (*below*) works on a section of the Orange & Alexandria torn up during a raid near Catlett's Station, Virginia, by General Jeb Stuart's Confederate cavalry on August 22, 1862. It took Haupt's men only two days to restore traffic on the line. Such repairs were speeded by the simple track-splicing device at left, which could hold together two segments of a broken rail.

Ingenious Ways of Undoing the Damage

Herman Haupt proved just as ingenious at repairing damage done by Confederate raiders as he was at plotting ways to demolish Confederate trackage. Mobilizing his wondrously efficient Construction Corps, he invented methods of straightening sabotaged rails, swiftly repairing and relaying ripped-up track, and salvaging derailed Federal rolling stock.

Under Haupt's energetic direction, the Construction Corps grew in size and scope as well as skill. Originally operating only in Virginia, it was active in Tennessee by 1863, helping keep open supply lines for Federal armies fighting there. During the last years of the War — when it numbered more than 10,000 workmen — the corps performed prodigious feats of bridge reconstruction and relaid hundreds of miles of track destroyed by retreating Confederates.

A shiny locomotive *(below, right)* stands ready to haul a pair of badly damaged engines to Haupt's Alexandria repair shops, along with a flatcar loaded with twisted rails.

101

Near an old rail tunnel leading to the Alexandria wharves, two teams of workers plying four-by-four beams heave on a length of rail to straighten it. A warp in the rail is still visible at right.

Tightening a portable jackscrew with a lever, a worker finishes straightening a rail. The looped tracks were bent around trees by Confederates.

Beside their guard post burrowed into the railroad embankment, men of the 164th New York Zouaves watch over a stretch of the Orange & Alexandria.

Methods of Foiling Confederate Saboteurs

Haupt also turned his imagination to the problem of guarding his tracks and bridges against attack. One invention was the tiny pontoon raft *(right)*, used to inspect the undersides of bridges for signs of sabotage.

In addition, Haupt badgered the various army commanders into stationing troops to guard the tracks. And he developed fortified bridges — formidable structures calculated to give any raider pause. But what truly discouraged the Confederates was the Construction Corps' ability to rebuild wrecked bridges and tracks seemingly overnight. It took the corps less than five days to reconstruct a 780-foot span over Georgia's Chattahoochie River in 1864. And when the Confederates fighting in Georgia that same year destroyed 35 miles of track and several bridges in a series of raids, the Construction Corps restored the line to full operation in a mere 13 days.

Brigadier General Haupt tests one of his own rafts, a crude platform atop two inflated rubber tubes about eight feet long and 10 inches in diameter. "A boat can be made of these," he wrote, "by running poles through the loops and then placing sticks across." Haupt said that a spy might deflate the tubes and carry them hidden under his overcoat.

The Cumberland River Bridge, near Nashville, Tennessee, bristles with wooden guard posts from which defenders could fire on enemy raiders.

The Backcountry Warriors

"In general my purpose was to threaten and harass the enemy on the border and in this way compel him to withdraw troops from his front to guard the line of the Potomac and Washington. This would greatly diminish his offensive power."

JOHN S. MOSBY, CONFEDERATE PARTISAN COMMANDER

"In no other way," wrote Abraham Lincoln on February 17, 1863, "does the enemy give us so much trouble, at so little expense to himself, as by the raids of rapidly moving small bodies of troops (largely, if not wholly, mounted), harassing and discouraging loyal residents, supplying themselves with provisions, clothing, horses, and the like, surprising and capturing small detachments of our forces, and breaking our communications."

It was to the partisans that the President somberly referred — those roving bands of irregulars who operated behind Federal lines with a disruptive power that belied their numbers. And Lincoln's assessment of their prowess was shared by his top commanders, among them General Philip Sheridan, who wrote in his memoirs, "During the entire campaign, I had been annoyed by guerrilla bands under such partisan chiefs as Mosby, White, Gilmore, McNeill and others, and this had considerably depleted my line-of-battle strength, necessitating as it did large escorts for my supply-trains."

Sheridan was particularly hard-hit. Assigned in 1864 to command Union forces in northern Virginia, the recently created state of West Virginia and much of Maryland, he had 48,000 men to deal with a threadbare Southern army of fewer than 9,000. Yet Sheridan was compelled to detach so many thousands of his troops to guard against the partisans who constantly assailed his lines of communication that, by his own estimate, the number of men he had for combat duty was much closer to that of the enemy.

In the forefront of the partisans were the four men whose names became familiar to Sheridan: John Singleton Mosby, a mite of a man who made up for his lack of size with a pair of Navy Colts that loomed large in his delicate hands; sleepy-eyed Elijah V. (Lige) White, whose men fought like wild Indians and came to be called "the Comanches"; Harry Gilmor, a beefy, boastful Marylander whose pet bloodhound was said to accompany him on raids; and John Hanson (Hanse) McNeill, a kindly, middle-aged farmer who was as likely as not to offer a captured Unionist a slug of applejack even while covering him with a double-barreled shotgun.

These men were heirs to a Revolutionary tradition. During the American War of Independence, few military leaders so captured popular imagination — especially in his native South — as Francis Marion, the elusive South Carolinian whose hit-and-run tactics once provoked a British officer to exclaim: "As for this damned old fox, the devil himself could not catch him!" Now, soon after the outbreak of the Civil War, as bands of partisans began springing up in the states threatened by Federal invasion, partisan chieftains vied for Marion's mantle, taking for themselves his honored title — Swamp Fox — or giving their riders such names as "the Swamp Rats."

The partisan warfare was particularly Confederate. Most of the Civil War was

Wearing rough woodsmen's clothes instead of their usual uniforms, two Confederate partisans fire from the cover of rocks at Federal troops on the riverbank below them. Union regulars deeply resented having to fight men in civilian dress who could melt into the population. "It is not surprising that our people get exasperated at such men," wrote General Henry Halleck, "and shoot them down when they can."

seasons. They appeared in tiny bands or, sometimes, in groups of several hundred. They swooped out of nowhere onto every sort of target — a wagon train, an enemy outpost, even a Federal general asleep in bed.

At first the partisans were compelled to operate without official sanction. In May 1861 the Richmond *Dispatch* was urging that the Virginia countryside be "made to swarm with our guerrillas" who would use "double-barreled fowling pieces loaded with buckshot." Yet the Confederate government was reluctant to sponsor armed groups over which it could exercise little control. Early in 1862, Confederate Secretary of War Judah P. Benjamin declared, "Guerrilla companies are not recognized as part of the military organization of the Confederate States, and cannot be authorized by this department."

It remained for the state of Virginia to clear the official way. To answer rising public demand, the state legislature on March 27, 1862, authorized at least 10 companies of "rangers and scouts" to be formed for operations within Union-occupied counties of the state. Generally subject to orders from Virginia's Governor, these raiders were to "give the greatest annoyance to the enemy."

Just one month after Virginia took the lead, the Confederate Congress passed a Partisan Ranger Act that called for the formal organization of companies, battalions and regiments of partisans who would receive the same uniforms and pay, and be entitled to the same rations and other allowances as regular soldiers.

And the Confederate Congress added a distinctive feature: Under the new law, guerrillas were to be paid for the full value of any arms or ammunition that they captured from

fought on Southern soil, and it was in the occupied areas of the Confederacy that guerrilla activity naturally evolved. Familiar with every mountain trail and woodland nook in their own domain, partisans were experts at striking, scattering and melting into the countryside — eluding vastly superior enemy forces. To Union commanders, perhaps the most nightmarish aspect of the partisan war was its lack of predictability. The guerrillas would attack by night or by day, in all

the enemy and delivered to a designated Confederate quartermaster. Meant as a lure for enlistment in partisan service, the provision turned out to be so attractive that the guerrilla outfits were flooded with recruits at the expense of the regular armies.

Their independence aside, partisan units were raised much in the same way as regiments for the regular army: A local citizen — usually prominent — would muster a group of volunteers and obtain a colonel's commission from Richmond. Under his aegis, lower officers would be elected and, thereafter, a cadre of men would take up the soldier's life in the field: drilling, bivouacking — and fighting. The partisans, of course, fought on their own and seldom had the support of friendly military units. So on major raids against the enemy, a partisan company often gained the help of local civilians; after the operation, the citizens would fade back into the population until called on again.

Partisan activity had been under way for months by the time the Confederate government got around to authorizing such independent units. And the men who would become the Confederacy's foremost partisan leaders had begun to appear on the scene.

On August 30, 1861, a young rider from Baltimore stole through Federal picket lines, spurred his horse into the shallow water of the Potomac and crossed the river into Virginia. His name was Harry Gilmor, and he was the 24-year-old scion of a prosperous shipping and mercantile family whose sympathies lay with the South. As a member of one of Baltimore's secessionist militia outfits, Gilmor had already been arrested by Union authorities and held for several weeks before being released. Now Gil-

mor was seeking a partisan's life.

He was determined to serve with Turner Ashby, a gentleman farmer who was making a reputation as the leader of a partisan regiment operating around Winchester. Ashby, a dashing figure whose guerrillas had plagued Union lines of communication in the lower Shenandoah Valley, would soon be deemed too valuable to be left romping about the countryside. Ashby and his men would be absorbed into Stonewall Jackson's Army of the Valley, and it was as a brigadier general and Jackson's chief of cavalry that Ashby would die fighting on June 6, 1862.

But in that first summer of the War, Ashby's magnetism drew young adventurers like Gilmor from afar. Gilmor found Ashby and some of his men relaxing on the lawn of a home near Charles Town, just north of Winchester. The brash Gilmor bragged of his marksmanship, avowing he could even shoot an apple off a man's head. Since there were no volunteers as apple holders, Gilmor contented himself with popping away expertly at other small targets. Before the day was over, he was enlisted as one of Ashby's riders, and that night he was sent out on his first mission with a small scouting party led by 29-year-old Elijah V. White.

Like Gilmor, White belonged to a Maryland family of means, and he had a nose for trouble. He went west in the 1850s and, as a member of a company of Missouri militia, got involved in the Kansas fighting against John Brown's abolitionists. After returning East, White settled near Leesburg, Virginia, joined the local cavalry and helped suppress

Major Harry Gilmor's inordinate vanity sometimes obscured his talents as a guerrilla chief. Shrewd, tenacious and flamboyant, he liked to ride into battle bearing packets of love letters from devoted women. His boast was that he always fought "fairly and in good faith."

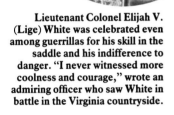

Lieutenant Colonel Elijah V. (Lige) White was celebrated even among guerrillas for his skill in the saddle and his indifference to danger. "I never witnessed more coolness and courage," wrote an admiring officer who saw White in battle in the Virginia countryside.

Brown's uprising at Harpers Ferry in 1859. By the start of the Civil War, White was a corporal; but when an officer he disliked took command of the company, White enlisted as a private in Ashby's outfit. While home on furlough in October 1861, not long after he and Harry Gilmor went on the night patrol, White was in a buggy with a young woman when he heard gunfire from the nearby Potomac. Without a moment's hesitation, White took off for the fighting (what happened to his companion went unrecorded) and volunteered. In what became known as the Battle of Ball's Bluff, White distinguished himself and was recommended for a commission. Yet when he went to Richmond to sign up, he was told that no vacancy existed in the regular army. Thwarted, White asked for permission — which was quickly granted — to raise an independent company for service in Loudoun County.

By year's end he had recruited no more than 15 men. As spring approached, White's little group watched disconsolately as General Joseph E. Johnston, commander of the Confederate forces in northern Virginia, burned his supplies in preparation for a withdrawal. Wrote one of the men: "The morning air was dark and heavy with the gloom of destruction which brooded over the land."

Remaining behind, White was soon in the element of the true partisan — cut off from the regular army and operating in an area controlled by enemy forces. He and his riders soon struck, raiding the village of Salem, a depot on the Manassas Gap Railroad, a line that ran from Manassas to Strasburg, Virgin-

ia. They succeeded in driving off the guard and in seizing the equipment wagons of the 28th Pennsylvania Infantry Regiment.

All too soon, however, White discovered the perils of being a partisan in a border area. In May 1862, while returning from a scouting mission west of Massanutten Ridge, White and his men were attacked by civilians who mistook them for a Federal scouting party. During the fight that followed, White was shot near the right eye. Thinking himself mortally wounded, he lay on his back, shouting encouragement to his men: "Do as I did — never surrender!"

As it happened, the wound did little permanent damage beyond causing a droop in White's right eyelid that gave him a decidedly sleepy look. Within a month he would be back in the saddle.

And as General Robert E. Lee advanced northward from the Rappahannock late in the summer of 1862, in a campaign that led to the battles of Second Bull Run and Antietam, White and his band were ready to help.

Under the terms of Congress' authorization, partisans were to place themselves at the disposal of regular army commanders, especially for major campaigns. During Lee's northward movement, White more than lived up to his obligations. His first mission was to distract Federal attention from Stonewall Jackson's corps as it slipped from the Rappahannock into the rear of the Union army led by Major General John Pope.

As Jackson left the Confederate line on the Rappahannock, White's partisans rode along for a while. Then they peeled off and galloped hard for Loudoun County, their home ground, on a raid that would help divert attention from Jackson and also enable White's men to settle some personal scores.

In Loudoun, Unionists had formed their own partisan outfit under a local miller and railroad stationmaster named Samuel C. Means, and the group had been busily harassing the county's secessionist sympathizers. To White, it was unthinkable that enemy guerrillas should dominate his own domain, and he had declared at the beginning of his expedition that he meant "to whip Means' men, no matter how many."

White came upon Means's 50 irregulars as they gathered in the courtyard of a Baptist meeting house near the village of Waterford around dawn on August 27; Means himself was at his nearby home. The first shots from White's men sent the Unionists scurrying into the meeting house. But as the firing through the windows grew hotter, some of the defenders judged their position untenable. The Confederates, as one of White's men recalled, were soon treated to the sight of Means's men "leaping from the windows and making the fastest kind of time."

Some Unionists, however, remained in the sturdy little church and put up a stout resistance. After about three hours, Means's men proposed to surrender on the condition that they be paroled. Since White's ammunition was running low, he was only too happy to agree. After their success — richer by 56 captured horses and about 200 small arms — the partisans rode into Leesburg, where they were regaled with cake and wine by the town's ladies. For good measure, the women prayed that "the God of Battles defend and encircle you all in the arms of love."

While White's raid was helping to distract Union attentions, Stonewall Jackson and his entire corps had passed through a mountain gap and looted and burned the enormous Union supply depot at Manassas Junction.

Jackson's troops had then taken position in John Pope's rear, and thus they precipitated the Second Battle of Bull Run.

In the Antietam Campaign that followed, White's partisans rode with Lee and scouted around Harpers Ferry. During a rearguard skirmish near Leesburg on September 17, White was severely wounded by a bullet that entered beneath his shoulder blade. Years later he recalled: "The Union captain who had shot me came up and asked if there was anything he could do for me. I told him I would like some water. He gave me a drink and then muttered, 'I hope you will forgive me.' I thought I was going to die and, do you know, I forgave that damn yankee."

Also running afoul of bad fortune during the Antietam Campaign was White's old scouting companion, Harry Gilmor. Since spring, Gilmor had been scouting for Stonewall Jackson. And as Lee's army entered Maryland, Gilmor was riding with it; he was determined to use the invasion as an occasion for visiting his family in Baltimore.

Seven miles short of the city, Gilmor turned off toward a friend's home which, by sheer bad luck, was at that very moment surrounded by Union soldiers and policemen who were raiding the place in search of contraband. When Gilmor came galloping out of the night, he was immediately taken prisoner. "I was treated very rudely by my captors," Gilmor wrote later. He especially resented being forced to walk all the way into Baltimore, where he spent the next five months in prison before being exchanged.

While White and Gilmor were temporarily absent from the scene, the guerrilla movement grew apace, spurred by the Partisan Ranger Act. By September 12, 1862, the Confederate War Department could report

Confederates pursuing Union raiders aboard the *General* started on foot at Big Shanty, then picked up successive locomotives at Etowah Station, Kingston and Adairsville. The Union men left two cars near Resaca and a third just past Tunnel Hill, Georgia. The *General* ran out of fuel two miles north of Ringgold after covering 87 miles.

James Andrews' greatest asset as a Union raider, said an admirer, was that he resembled "the ideal Southern officer." A Georgia stationmaster said of Andrews, "I'd as soon have suspected Mr. Jefferson Davis."

A Run for Life on a Georgia Railroad

It was "the deepest scheme that ever emanated from the brains of Yankees," declared the *Southern Confederacy* in its issue of April 11, 1862. Certainly the Great Railroad Adventure, as the plot came to be called, was one of the more bizarre undertakings hatched by either side during the War.

As proposed by a contraband trader named James J. Andrews, the plan called for Federal raiders to penetrate into Georgia, seize a locomotive on the Western & Atlantic Railroad and race north, burning bridges on the line between Atlanta and Chattanooga, Tennessee. Thus isolated, Chattanooga would presumably fall easily to the Union forces advancing from the west.

Andrews recruited volunteers from an Ohio brigade in Tennessee. Dressed in civilian clothes, the men rendezvoused in Marietta, Georgia. Sixteen were on hand at dawn on April 12, 1862, when a northbound passenger train pulled by the locomotive *General* steamed into Marietta. The raiders presented tickets and climbed aboard.

When passengers and crew got off for breakfast at a whistle stop known as Big Shanty, Andrews and his men swiftly un-

The 25-ton *General* was one of a class of eight-wheel, wood-burning locomotives. With five-foot driving wheels, it could go more than 60 miles an hour.

Steaming in reverse with crew members clinging on, the *Texas* pushes the last car dropped by the *General*. Although several raiders recalled that the car was burning, others said that they failed to set it aflame.

With bell clanging, Confederate pursuers race after the *General*. Joining the chase at the village of Calhoun were 10 soldiers of the 1st Georgia Confederate Volunteers

coupled all but three boxcars behind the locomotive and took off. The raiders raced northward, pausing only to cut telegraph wires and to make a few futile efforts to wreck the tracks.

In hot pursuit came railroad employees led by Conductor William A. Fuller, who was so enraged at the theft of his train that he had started chasing on foot. The one-sided race gradually evened out: First the pursuers commandeered a push car and then three successive locomotives — the *Yonah*, the *William R. Smith* and finally the *Texas*. The last of these was headed south, but the pursuers threw it into reverse and continued the chase going backward.

Forced onto a siding by unexpected southbound traffic on the single line of track, the raiders lost an hour and saw their lead dwindle to almost nothing. They had no time for their primary mission — to burn bridges. The fleeing raiders desperately dropped crossties on the tracks and uncoupled first one boxcar and then two others as impediments to their pursuers. But the Confederate locomotives simply pushed the dropped cars ahead of them, recalled one raider, and came "screaming along after us." Near Ringgold, the *General* ran out of fuel, with the *Texas* close on its heels. The raiders took to the woods. The eight-hour chase was over.

Within a week, everybody in the Andrews party was captured. Andrews himself and seven others, selected at random, were hanged. Eight escaped from prison and reached Union lines. The rest remained in Confederate prisons until they were exchanged in March 1863.

With their engine out of fuel and the pursuing *Texas* in view, the Federal raiders abandon the *General* and flee for their lives. "When the order was given by Andrews," said one raider, "the boys lit out like a flock of quail."

that six partisan regiments, nine battalions and 24 companies were operating in Virginia and in Union-held coastal pockets as far south as Florida. Among the partisans, by the end of 1862, were men led by John Hanson McNeill and John S. Mosby.

Hanse McNeill was a study in paradox. Although he opposed secession, he willingly went to war for the Confederacy. A plain, no-frills farmer, he nonetheless affected an ebony plume that perched jauntily on his black, broad-brimmed hat. And, not least, he was a fierce fighter who always carried a double-barreled shotgun; but he much preferred trickery to killing.

McNeill was born and reared in Hardy County in the wild isolation of the South Branch Valley in northwestern Virginia. After moving to Missouri, he prospered as a livestock breeder and an authority on Shorthorn cattle. During the early months of the Civil War, while commanding a Confederate militia company, McNeill was captured and taken to St. Louis. But he eventually escaped, made his way to Richmond and, in the late summer of 1862, successfully sought permission to raise a company of partisans in his native Hardy County — within striking range of a long stretch of the Baltimore & Ohio Railroad (B & O).

The B & O was crucial to the Union war effort. Starting at Baltimore, the line linked up with the Potomac River and followed it westward across the Blue Ridge to the Alleghenies and thence to the Ohio River. The railroad transported not only troops but coal, grain and other precious commodities from the Midwest to the Northeast.

Unfortunately for the Union, the B & O was uniquely vulnerable. For three quarters of its length, it ran through Virginia, and every mile of the line lay in territory that had been slaveholding when the War began. The rail therefore presented a singular target for Confederate guerrillas.

Hanse McNeill, with his son, Jesse, riding as one of his lieutenants, set about bedeviling the B & O. At the time, the defense of the line had been placed in the hands of a long-suffering Union brigadier general named Benjamin F. Kelley. Known to his troops as Old Ben, he was a large, deeply religious man who deserved a better fate than the War would grant him. At least in part because of his endless skirmishes with the guerrillas, it was later said of Kelley that he did more fighting while making less history than any other general in the Union's service.

To carry out his thankless task, Kelley at first had been assigned mostly infantry, which he shuffled back and forth by rail in a desperate, and futile, effort to anticipate the places where guerrillas were likely to strike. Clearly, what he most needed was cavalry to pursue the partisans to their lairs; and finally, in response to his repeated pleas, there arrived the crack 1st New York Cavalry.

As one of their first orders of business, the New Yorkers were divided into groups and sent to root out the partisans who infested a stretch of the nearby Allegheny Mountains. Hardly had the troopers entered the wilderness than the men of one party were captured by McNeill and his partisan band. The legend of Hanse McNeill began when he cordially offered the Union commander a swig of the drink distilled from local apples.

John Hanson (Hanse) McNeill's greatest gifts as a Confederate raider were his unflappable calm and his countryman's shrewd knowledge of the mountainous terrain where he operated in northwestern Virginia. Union General Philip Sheridan judged him "the most daring and dangerous of all the bushwhackers in this section of the country."

Before long, the clever McNeill showed that he also possessed an understanding of the psychology of the enemy's soldiers. As he realized, most of them were mere boys, taken up by the Union Army and cast down far from their homes in a remote and joyless region. Split into small detachments to guard the railroad's bridges, water towers and way stations, they maintained their lonely vigil never knowing if the night's next shadow might turn out to be a guerrilla bent on murder. All too understandably, their morale stood at rock bottom.

And so, Hanse McNeill, preparing to attack a Federal wagon train outside Romney — a key town near the B & O, which was said to have changed hands no fewer than 56 times during the War — shouted to the Union youngsters: "I don't want to hurt you. Throw down your arms and I'll parole every devil of you and you can go home."

McNeill's forlorn opponents leaped at the chance; with only 24 men in his own band, Hanse took 72 Federals out of the War, at least temporarily. The tactic was so successful that he adopted it on a wholesale basis, leaving stacks of blank paroles, all duly signed, with local farmers. Any Union soldier anxious to go home could get one simply by trading coffee, sugar or some other desirable commodity in exchange.

Through such tactics Hanse McNeill made himself invaluable to the Confederacy's guerrillas. And, by the beginning of 1863, the partisan ranks would be strengthened beyond measure by a commander without peer — John Singleton Mosby.

"Quiet to quick bosoms is a hell," Mosby once wrote, quoting Lord Byron, and Mosby possessed nothing if not a quick bosom. A native of Virginia's Nelson and Albemarle Counties, Mosby had been a frail, consumptive youth who attended the University of Virginia — until his hair-trigger temper got him in trouble. During an argument, a fellow student made what Mosby thought a "disagreeable allegation," so Mosby hauled out a revolver and wounded the boy.

Mosby was expelled, and was taken before a judge who sentenced him to a year in jail for "unlawful shooting." He turned his incarceration to his own advantage, however, by persuading the prosecuting attorney to lend him some law books. Soon after his release, Mosby hung up his own shingle. By 1858, he was married and had settled into the tranquil life of a lawyer in Bristol, Virginia, on the Tennessee border.

The Civil War disrupted this tranquillity. Although Mosby opposed secession, he quickly answered the call of his native state, explaining: "Virginia is my mother, God bless her! I can't fight against my mother, can I?" Always a romantic — who carried volumes by Shakespeare, Plutarch, Byron and others in his saddlebag — he naturally enlisted in the cavalry.

At 27, Mosby was an unlikely sort of trooper. Still frail, he weighed a mere 125 pounds. Worse, he was an indifferent horseman. Yet he soon found that war is a great equalizer. "I was glad to see," he said later, "that little men were a match for the big men through being armed."

But Mosby also found that military life, whatever its virtues, was laced with disciplinary requirements for which he had little patience. By February 1862, he had ascended from private to lieutenant and regimental adjutant, 1st Virginia Cavalry. But he chafed under the discipline, and he once outraged Colonel Fitzhugh Lee, a West Pointer and a stickler for military punctilio, by calling a bugle a horn. "Sir!" cried Lee, "if I ever again hear you calling that bugle a horn, I will put you under arrest!"

Mosby's days as a staff officer were numbered. When Fitzhugh Lee, whom he detested, assumed command of the 1st Virginia Cavalry, Mosby resigned his commission and volunteered his services as a scout to Brigadier General Jeb Stuart. In that capacity, he distinguished himself in June 1862, during Stuart's famous ride around General McClellan's Federal army in the Peninsular Campaign — so much so that Stuart cited Mosby's exploits as "a shining record of daring and usefulness."

Mosby was soon able to make another contribution, though not in a way that he intended. On July 19 Mosby was dozing in the shade at Beaver Dam Station north of Richmond, waiting for a train to take him home for a brief visit, when a contingent of Federal cavalry burst on the scene and captured him. He was taken to Washington, held in the Old Capitol Prison for 10 days and then placed aboard a truce boat with other prisoners who were to be shipped South and exchanged.

The steamer made its way down the Potomac to Hampton Roads and waited there for a few days for clearance to proceed up the James River to Richmond. Mosby could not help noticing a great number of Federal transports crammed with troops lying at Newport News. Mosby already had correctly guessed that the captain of the truce ship was a Confederate sympathizer, and a discreet inquiry of him produced some electrifying information: On board the Federal ships was General Ambrose Burnside's army, on its way from North Carolina to reinforce General John Pope's army around Manassas. As soon as he was released, Mosby made his way to General Robert E. Lee and told him the crucial news. Shortly thereafter Lee began his advance north, bound for Bull Run and later Antietam Creek.

Still, Mosby chafed. As a youth, his idol had been Francis Marion, the original Swamp Fox; as a man during the early months of the Civil War, his hero was Turner Ashby. Now Mosby yearned to be a partisan leader himself. Finally he won his case with Stuart; in December 1862, after completing a cavalry raid in Fairfax County in northern Virginia, Stuart left Mosby behind with nine men and permission to start operating as a partisan.

This was Mosby's chance, and he made the most of it. Within a few days, Union officers in the area began reporting a series of mystifying nighttime raids against their outposts by riders who approached in stealth, attacked, then vanished as suddenly as they had come, scooping up seven Federal prisoners in one wild rush, five in another. By January 17, Mosby had taken 22 prisoners. In response, Colonel Percy Wyndham, a British soldier of fortune and a formidable Union cavalry commander, began dispatching large search parties to ferret out the guerrillas. Mosby, however, could soon gloat that the Union soldiers found nothing but "old farmers in bed. And when they returned to camp, they often found that we had paid them a visit in their absence."

Before long, Mosby and Wyndham were engaged in a personal feud, in the course of which Wyndham made the mistake of calling Mosby a common horse thief. Mosby determined to avenge the slur against his sacred honor. So began one of the most spectacular episodes of the partisan war.

As he leaped on his horse in Loudoun County on the rainy night of March 8, 1863, John S. Mosby announced: "I shall mount the stars tonight or sink lower than plummet ever sounded." With that dramatic declaration, Mosby led 29 men into the dripping darkness toward Fairfax Court House, 25 miles distant, where Percy Wyndham had established his headquarters. Their mission: to capture the insolent Englishman.

All night they rode, silently gliding through enemy picket lines, arriving at the outskirts of their destination before dawn and taking a few prisoners, who told them that Wyndham had unexpectedly been sum-

moned to Washington. Mosby's disappointment was greatly lessened, however, when a captured Federal let slip that a bigger catch —Brigadier General Edwin H. Stoughton —was slumbering in a nearby house.

The scion of a wealthy Vermont family, Stoughton had been, at the age of 24, the youngest general in the Union service. Now, at 25, he was something of a dandy, who delighted in entertaining the ladies and politicians who came to Fairfax from Washington. On this particular night he had played host at a champagne party, and at the moment of Mosby's arrival he was sleeping off the effects of his revelries.

Confederate guerrilla leader John S. Mosby stands second from left among officers of the 43rd Battalion of Partisan Rangers. So many of Mosby's men came from the Loudoun County area of Virginia that one of them claimed, "Scarcely a family in all that section did not have some members in Mosby's command."

Forcing his way at gunpoint into Stoughton's lodging place, Mosby hurried upstairs and found the general snoring loudly. Lifting the man's nightshirt, Mosby smartly slapped Stoughton's bare buttocks, ordering: "Get up, General, and come with me."

Rousing himself, the befuddled Stoughton looked up and saw a stranger bent over him. "What is this?" he cried angrily. "Do you know who I am, sir?"

"I reckon I do, General," replied the intruder. "Did you ever hear of Mosby?"

"Yes, have you caught him?"

"No, but he has caught you."

And that ended Edwin H. Stoughton's brief, inglorious military career. Along with two captains and 30 enlisted men, Stoughton was taken away by the Confederates. A few months later, after being released, he resigned from the Federal Army.

Mosby's exploit raised a cheer from none other than Robert E. Lee, who wrote with rare exuberance: "Hurrah for Mosby!" From the Union's point of view, it remained for President Lincoln to put the episode into perspective. When told that Mosby had netted not only a brigadier general but also 58 horses, the President murmured reflectively: "Well, I'm sorry for that. I can make new brigadier generals, but I can't make horses."

In the summer of 1863, after the Confederate victory at Chancellorsville, the war in the East neared another crescendo as General Lee, on the Rappahannock, prepared to invade the North. The guerrillas stepped up their activities, Mosby foremost.

Late in May, Mosby and his men made their way to Catlett's Station, Virginia, on the Orange & Alexandria Railroad; working from the cover of a stand of trees, they dis-

In Pursuit of a Partisan Chief

"Mosby is an old rat and has a great many holes," wrote Union Colonel Charles Russell Lowell after an extensive search failed to reveal the whereabouts of the guerrilla leader in August of 1863. The complaint was not an unfamiliar one to the Federal cavalrymen who made the pursuit of John Singleton Mosby virtually a full-time occupation. Prominent among Mosby's pursuers were the 2nd Massachusetts Cavalry under Colonel Lowell and the 13th New York Cavalry under Colonel Henry Sanford Gansevoort. These two regiments had been posted outside Washington and charged with defending the capital and waging war against the Confederate guerrillas that were infesting northern Virginia.

For the most part, the Federal campaign to combat the raiders consisted of abortive cavalry responses to Mosby's swift strikes and small, bloody clashes in which the Union

Colonel Henry S. Gansevoort (*center*) stands with his staff at Prospect Hill, Virginia. He reported gloomily that "the whole country is full of guerrillas."

Troopers of the 13th New York Cavalry line up in battle formation during a review at Prospect Hill. Colonel Gansevoort sits on his horse at the extreme right in the

horsemen often were defeated. On July 6, 1864, for instance, at Mount Zion Church near Aldie, Virginia, 40 Union cavalrymen were killed and 57 taken prisoner when Mosby's guerrillas came "swooping down like Indians," in the words of one shaken survivor. Colonel Lowell, who was an excellent officer, summarized the action bluntly: "I have only to report a perfect rout and a chase for five to seven miles."

The Union cavalry suffered almost as severe a setback in a clash with Mosby at Fairfax Station, and again near Falls Church. The deadly war of attrition went on day and night:

"I lost two men last week," reported Colonel Gansevoort on one occasion. "In the dark the enemy crawled upon them when they were on post as pickets." He acknowledged that he was "wearied of the thankless task of fighting guerrillas," and then added: "Mosby is continually around us."

The campgrounds of the 2nd Massachusetts Cavalry near Washington are surrounded by a stockade as a protection against guerrilla infiltration.

oreground, and the regimental musicians are mounted on white horses in the rear.

Union General Edwin Stoughton was so vain that when he was kidnapped by Mosby from his bed at the settlement of Fairfax Court House, he astonished the guerrilla chief by "dressing meticulously before a mirror." In the view below, Federal cavalrymen gather before the courthouse near the place where Stoughton was seized.

placed a rail—and waited. It was not long before a train bearing supplies for General Hooker's army, camped north of the Rappahannock, came rumbling by; suddenly the train lurched and, in a cacophony of screaming metal, stopped. Down the tracks, Mosby's gunners wheeled out a little mountain howitzer—which the Confederates had captured at Ball's Bluff—and began banging away, causing a huge hiss of steam as one of its balls crashed through the locomotive's boiler. Then the partisans came swarming out of a copse of trees, gathered up as much of the train's cargo as they could carry and galloped away.

In hot pursuit came men from three Union cavalry regiments. The chase halted when the 40 or so guerrillas faced the howitzer around and let go with a charge of grapeshot. After a brief, whirling, hand-to-hand fight, Mosby signaled with a blast from a whistle he carried for that purpose, and in the best partisan style, his men scattered in all directions—to reassemble and share their prizes later. They were forced to leave behind their howitzer, but they had looted a train that contained, among other supplies, a quantity of shad, a delicacy the Virginians found very much to their taste.

A few days later, Lee put his army in motion northward. As the troops moved, the partisans struck their enemy repeatedly. Far off to the west, acting as shield for Lee's left flank, Hanse McNeill drove the Federals out of Romney and held the place for a week. Even after being dislodged from the town by Union forces superior to his in number, McNeill kept hammering away at the B & O Railroad; he wrecked the trestle over the Great Cacapon River, burned the water stations at Rockwell's and Willet's Run, and

destroyed the supervisor's office and other facilities at Sir John's Run.

On June 10, meanwhile, Mosby gathered his men at Rector's Crossroads and announced that the War Department had officially designated them the 43rd Battalion of Partisan Rangers. Then, in high spirits, Mosby's Rangers followed their chief across the Potomac into Maryland to burn a Union camp at Seneca Mills. At one point, the Federals pursuing Mosby surrounded a house where he was thought to be staying, searched the place and came up empty-handed. After they departed, Mosby climbed down from the tree in which he had been hiding in his boots and underwear.

At Gettysburg, in July 1863, the Confederates reached the apex of their war effort. Although hardly anyone fully realized it at

the time, the melancholy recessional had begun when General Lee's defeated army moved South from Pennsylvania. This too was the period when a prophecy by President Lincoln would be fulfilled. "As the rebellion grows weaker," he wrote in 1863, "it will run more and more to guerrillaism."

As the grayclad troops withdrew southward, officials of the Baltimore & Ohio took stock and reported that owing to attacks, the line had been in full operation for only six months and six days during the previous 12 months. Now, as the Union forces moved ever more deeply into Virginia, their lines of communication were being stretched, and an even greater burden fell on the railroads — not only on the B & O but also on the Orange & Alexandria Railroad, which had become the direct line of supply for a host of 100,000 men and 8,000 horses.

The partisans swarmed against these lines of communication. So numerous were the attacks that in the spring of 1864, General Franz Sigel was compelled to station more than 22,000 men along the tracks of the B & O. Yet these forces were not enough to halt the attacks. Stopping the guerrillas was a task that one Federal officer compared to shooting mosquitoes with a rifle. It was, he said, "very smashing to the little insect — if you hit him."

By this time Lige White had recovered from his severe wound at Antietam, but his days as a partisan leader had come to an end. In the winter of 1862, White had been asked by Confederate officials to transfer with his command to the regular army. White approved of the move, and although some of his men at first protested, he and his battalion were assigned to duty under General Stonewall Jackson and spent the rest of

the War fighting alongside regular units.

Harry Gilmor, who had been exchanged before Gettysburg, was back in the field and seeking to make up lost time. Unfortunately, he would reveal a dark side during the remainder of his career. More than once, Gilmor would allow discipline among his partisans to relax dangerously, and even let them succumb to outright robbery.

Early in 1864, Gilmor and 28 men set up a barricade across the Baltimore & Ohio tracks near Martinsburg, in what was now West Virginia, and waited for a train to come along. It happened to be an express out of Baltimore, bearing sick and wounded Union soldiers being furloughed home, and a number of civilians. As the train reached the barricade and screeched to a stop, Gilmor's guerrillas leaped aboard and began robbing the passengers. Reported the Baltimore *American:* "Even their pocket knives and toothpicks did not escape the plunderers."

According to one Northern account, the thieves departed with nine gold watches, two silver watches, 50 to 60 hats, 30 overcoats, 100 revolvers and $100,000 in cash. The last item was doubtless an exaggeration, but the fact remained that Gilmor's men had trespassed beyond the line that separated legitimate partisan warfare from thuggery.

Not long afterward they did it again. Near the Shenandoah Valley town of Strasburg, they pounced on a wagon train owned by Jewish merchants who were engaged in buying merchandise in Maryland for resale in Richmond. About $6,000, mainly in $20 gold pieces, was taken and one of the merchants was relieved of his Hebrew prayer book. Though Gilmor himself was not there, it was later reported that while in his cups he had bragged of planning the robbery.

The Wild Flight of Harry Gilmore

To avoid capture in northern Virginia, a Confederate guerrilla leader had to have nerve, quick reflexes and more than his share of luck. When commanding a ranger battalion in fighting around Darkesville in the late summer of 1864, Colonel Harry Gilmor was shot through the shoulder and collarbone and put out of action. A Confederate ambulance took him to a hospital in Winchester, where his wound was dressed. To convalesce, he stayed with a widowed friend named Mrs. O'Bannon. Cared for by his hostess's two nieces, Gilmor passed three weeks that he called "among the happiest of my life."

The idyll was interrupted by the defeat of Confederate forces outside Winchester on September 19. As the Confederate troops retreated through the town, Gilmor realized that he would probably be captured in bed by the Federals. He shouted to the nieces to bring him his trousers and hurried into the street wearing only his pants and a nightshirt. One of Gilmor's rangers, recognizing his leader, gave up his horse to let Gilmor escape. "I must have cut a sorry figure," Gilmor recalled, "tearing through the streets of Winchester without hat, coat or shoes, my naked feet hanging below the stirrups, which were too short for me!" But he got away to take his last guerrilla command, in West Virginia.

On a borrowed horse, Confederate partisan leader Harry Gilmor flees from the Federals in Winchester, Virginia.

The banditry of Gilmor's guerrillas set off an outcry in both the North and the South. Robert E. Lee declared that "such conduct is unauthorized and discreditable. Should any of the battalion be captured the enemy might claim to treat them as highway robbers." Ordered to stand court-martial for the train escapade, Gilmor insisted that his men had robbed the passengers while his back was turned. "This," he wrote piously in his memoirs, "was against my positive orders."

In any case, Gilmor was acquitted and he returned to duty. Yet the affair had left a foul taste in nearly everyone's mouth, and as the commanding officer responsible for the conduct of his men, Harry Gilmor had helped bring the entire partisan establishment into disrepute. Guerrillas, said one Confederate general, were "a terror to the citizens and an injury to the cause."

The Confederate government had been growing increasingly disenchanted with the partisans. Officials were concerned not only about the lawlessness, but also about the fact that many young men were joining the independent companies to avoid regular service, where they were most needed. Even generals such as Jeb Stuart and Robert E. Lee began to speak out against the partisan companies. "The evils resulting from their organization more than counterbalance the good they accomplish," Lee told Secretary of War James A. Seddon in January 1864. "I recommend that the law authorizing these partisan corps be abolished." The Confederate Congress took his advice, and on February 15, 1864, it repealed the Partisan Ranger Act. The new law abolished the independent companies, but in fact gave Seddon the right to make certain exceptions; after consulting with his generals, he granted Mosby and McNeill permission to continue their raiding.

For all that, the new legislation was a hollow gesture. At this stage of the War, the Confederate government had no means of enforcing the measure, and guerrilla bands of all stripes continued to operate.

In the spring of 1864, Hanse McNeill was based in the Alleghenies, around the town of Moorefield, and operating with deadly effectiveness. On the evening of May 3, 1864, he led 60 men from their bastion near the Lost River. They rode all night, trotting northward. Next day, by prudent partisan custom, they rested, hidden in the woods, and resumed their march when darkness fell once more. At dawn on March 5 they arrived at Bloomington Bridge, where the B & O crossed the Potomac just east of the Alleghenies. A mile and a half farther east lay Piedmont, a key depot and rail yard.

McNeill's guerrillas had only a few minutes to wait before an eastbound freight train rolled out of the mountains. Flagging it down, most of the partisans jumped aboard. With a partisan's revolver pressing against his temple, the engineer drove them past Union guards and delivered them in fine style to the heart of the B & O installations.

The partisans made quick work of the place. Explosions sounded, flames leaped high into the air, and the raiders departed as swiftly as they had come, racing westward on the horses that had been brought up behind the train. By the time a 75-man detail of Union reinforcements arrived from nearby New Creek, Piedmont was in ruins. Seven large buildings had burned, including machine shops, paint shops and enginehouses; 2,000 feet of track had been torn up; and nine locomotives and 22 freight cars had been destroyed. Meanwhile, a rear guard left at Bloomington had stopped and burned three more trains and captured 100 soldiers on board them—all without firing a shot.

McNeill's exploit produced an immediate reaction in Washington. To strengthen the railroad defenses, the War Department ordered reinforcements forward from Ohio and posted 11 regiments along the B & O in West Virginia. It was small wonder that General Kelley, the Union officer who was mainly responsible for the B & O's security, declared: "We must kill, capture or drive McNeill out of the country before we can expect quiet or safety along the line."

One of McNeill's own men did the job that Kelley so devoutly desired. Early in October, in a predawn raid on a Union-held bridge near Mount Jackson in the Shenandoah Valley, McNeill fell from his saddle, mortally wounded—shot, it was said, by a guerrilla McNeill had reprimanded for stealing chickens. Carried to a minister's house nearby, McNeill murmured to the grief-stricken men: "Good-by, boys. Go on and leave me. I've done all I can for my country."

Indeed he had: During his career as the partisan leader of a force that seldom numbered more than 65 guerrillas, McNeill had inflicted incalculable damage to the Baltimore & Ohio and had by one estimate captured 2,600 Federals.

It fell to McNeill's son, Jesse, to take charge of the company and write a glowing footnote to his father's story. In January 1865 Jesse McNeill learned that two Union generals were staying in the town of Cumberland, Maryland, within easy striking distance of his partisans. In the bitterly cold early-morning hours of the 21st, young McNeill led his men quietly into Cumberland, divided them into two groups and gave each its orders. One party stole into Barnum's Hotel and roughly awakened General Benjamin Kelley, the beleaguered protector of the Baltimore & Ohio. The other partisan contingent entered the Revere House and captured Major General George Crook as he slept. The partisans led their prisoners to waiting horses and escaped without incident.

Headlines soon trumpeted the episode, to the Union's embarrassment and the Confederacy's elation. General Crook himself complimented the younger McNeill, calling the raid "the most brilliant exploit of the war."

Just a few months after Hanse McNeill's death, the career of another partisan leader came to an abrupt end. When it came, the downfall of Harry Gilmor occurred quietly: In February 1865 Union scouts found his base near Romney and told General Sheridan, who sent 300 cavalrymen to the scene.

A few troopers entered the house where the guerrilla leader was sharing a bed with a woman. And for Harry Gilmor, caught in his night clothes, the War was over.

Thus by the spring of 1865, only John S. Mosby remained active as a guerrilla leader in Virginia. The little rider, who wore a flowing, crimson-lined cape, had carved out for himself an immense domain, a tract of rolling land between the Potomac and the Rappahannock that was known to friend and foe alike as "Mosby's Confederacy."

There, Mosby's men stayed constantly in motion. They had no regular base, they rarely stayed in one place long enough to call it a camp, and some of the men did not know how to pitch a tent. Moreover, as one of them recalled, "the idea of making coffee, frying bacon or soaking hardtack was never entertained. When we wanted to eat we stopped at a friendly farm house, or went into some little town and bought what we wanted."

In return for the hospitality offered them by the local population, Mosby's guerrillas frequently divided the bounty of their raids—livestock, foodstuffs and other supplies—with farmers and villagers who had done them favors. Rules of behavior toward those who offered shelter were rigidly enforced; for example, one man who broke into the milkhouse of his host was summarily sent to the regular army.

As for their weaponry, Mosby's men disdained the sabers so admired by the regular cavalry. The saber, said one of the men, was useless except as a "weapon with which to bat a refractory mule over the back." Instead of a sword, each man was armed with a pair of Colt .44 revolvers; the guerrillas practiced their marksmanship by firing bullets into a tree while riding past it at breakneck speed.

Whenever possible, Mosby so timed a raid as to attack in the darkness when his enemy was sleeping. This put surprise on his side and took advantage of his theory that an enemy soldier required five minutes to be fit to fight after being awakened.

"As a general thing," one guerrilla recalled, "our fights were fast and furious and quickly over."

But Mosby's lightning strikes were by no means haphazard affairs. A meticulous and highly secretive planner, Mosby was all business. On his way to a raid he concentrated fiercely: One of his men recalled riding alongside the chief "boot-leg to boot-leg for twenty miles. Not once did he look at me, nor one word did he utter in all that ride."

When it came time to carry out his plans, Mosby displayed a hardened resolve. Once,

when criticized for making railroad raids that might endanger civilian passengers, Mosby replied that he only attacked trains carrying soldiers. But, he added, "if there had been women and children, too, it would have been all the same to me. Those who travel on a road running through a military district must accept the risk of the accidents of war. It does not hurt people any more to be killed in a railroad wreck than having their heads knocked off by a cannon shot."

In the late summer of 1864 Robert E. Lee noted that during the previous six months Mosby had killed, wounded or captured 1,200 Federals and had taken more than 1,600 horses and mules, 230 head of cattle, and 85 wagons and ambulances. Yet Lee, by now under siege at Petersburg, pushed for more action against the enemy's railroads, and Mosby would soon have abundant opportunity to accommodate his commander.

At Petersburg, Lee relied heavily on the Virginia Central Railroad to bring food and fodder from southwestern Virginia by way of Charlottesville. For his part, General Ulysses S. Grant was obsessed with the idea of cutting that life line to Lee's forces. Grant determined that General Sheridan should move his forces from his base near Harpers Ferry and embark on an expedition to Charlottesville, where he could cut the Virginia Central. Grant repeatedly urged Sheridan to undertake the mission, but Sheridan begged off on grounds that his own supply line would be too stretched out to adequately provide for his men.

Finally, General Grant hit upon a solution—to repair the tracks of the little Manassas Gap Railroad, which ran from the Shenandoah Valley to a juncture with

Colonel John Singleton Mosby, mounted on a white horse *(below, right)*, is hailed by members of his command after they routed Union cavalry under Major William Forbes at Aldie, Virginia, on July 6, 1864. Union prisoners, some of them wounded, march in the center of the column, and the defeated Major Forbes sits at the right.

the Orange & Alexandria line at Manassas. Abandoned the previous year because of Confederate raids, the Manassas Gap line could be used to bring supplies from Alexandria, Virginia, to ease Sheridan's way south. And so, on October 3, a 150-man construction gang from Alexandria began work on the rails west of Manassas. Union engineers estimated that the job would take a week.

In fact, the repairs were never finished. On October 5, shots from two howitzers announced Mosby's presence. Union reinforcements were rushed to the scene, and 50

of them were captured in a whirlwind attack by the partisan riders. Soon another contingent of Federal troops on the railroad found the way blocked by the wreckage of a giant locomotive named *Grapeshot,* along with 12 cars loaded with construction materials. Mosby had caused the derailment. On the next morning, when construction officials went out to inspect the tracks, their train also was derailed and the railroad's assistant superintendent was killed.

During the days that followed, more trains were derailed, track was torn up and con-

Sitting erect in the saddle at left center, Colonel John S. Mosby receives a riderless thoroughbred named Coquette, given to him by the members of his command. The thoroughbred, which was bought with money taken in a train robbery in October 1864, became Mosby's favorite horse.

struction workers became the constant targets of snipers. In retaliation, Secretary of War Edwin Stanton ordered that every house within five miles of the tracks be burned unless its owner was "known to be friendly." The ugly job was done, but the guerrilla harassment continued unabated. Finally the railroad workers were recalled and the entire repair project was abandoned. To Grant's vast chagrin, Sheridan stayed where he was. A major military move had been prevented by a handful of guerrillas.

Then came a brief lull in the partisan activity—or so it seemed. A Union general was sufficiently encouraged to report to Chief of Staff Henry Halleck that two full days had gone by without a single attack anywhere by Mosby's men. Even as the news passed over the telegraph wires, it was learned that Mosby had struck again, this time at the B & O.

On the chilly night of October 13 Mosby took 84 men and—with a B & O timetable in his pocket—rode toward Duffield's, just west of Harpers Ferry. Arriving about 2:30 a.m. on the 14th, the guerrillas loosened a rail, settled down to wait for a train—and fell asleep. "We did not hear the train coming," Mosby recalled, "and I was aroused and astounded by an explosion and a crash.

"As we had displaced a rail, the engine had run off the track, the boiler burst, and the air was filled with red-hot cinders and escaping steam. A good description of the scene can be found in Dante's 'Inferno.'"

When they left the wreck, Mosby's guerrillas took with them more than $170,000 of payroll money meant for Union troops.

Two months later, in the twilight days of the Confederacy, Mosby's luck almost ran out. Twice before, he had been seriously

wounded, but he had rapidly recovered. (On the second occasion, while recuperating from a groin wound, he was said to have ridden on raids in a buggy.) Now, on the cold night of December 21, 1864, as sleet fell, he was dining on spareribs, rolls and coffee in the home of Fauquier County friends.

Outside, a 300-man Union cavalry detachment surrounded the house. As a corporal named Kane rode into the yard, he saw a small man in gray moving past a window in the house. Instantly, Kane fired his revolver and the bullet, smashing through the pane, struck John Mosby in the abdomen.

Mosby fell, in great pain and bleeding profusely. But somehow he managed to remove his jacket bearing his colonel's insignia, and he slung it under a bureau. After the Federals burst into the house, Mosby gave a false identity to a drunken major who questioned him. The Union cavalry departed, leaving Mosby to die in his own blood. He failed to oblige, and by March he was back in the saddle. In one of their last raids, Mosby's partisans galloped into Loudoun County and very nearly exterminated Lige White's old foes, the Federal guerrillas known as the Loudoun Rangers.

But the effort went for nothing. On April 9, 1865, the Army of Northern Virginia laid down its arms at Appomattox. Mosby, however, never surrendered his command formally. Instead, on April 21, he faced his men, who had been summoned to the crossroads hamlet of Salem. "I am now no longer your commander," he said. "Farewell."

Then, as they had so often done after a successful raid, the partisan chieftain and his men scattered back into the woods and hills of Mosby's Confederacy.

The Many Faces of John Mosby

Although John Singleton Mosby was the most elusive of the Confederate partisan leaders, he was perhaps the most photographed. A vain man who once remarked, "I did not affect to be indifferent to public praise," Mosby sat for a score or more of photographs commemorating the two and a half years of his wartime glory. Certain of the studio portraits are inaccurate — they show him carrying a sword that he never wore when campaigning, for example — but they also reveal the harrowing changes written on his face by wounds and the hardships of war.

CAPTAIN MOSBY IN THE SPRING OF 1863

MOSBY AS A MAJOR IN THE SUMMER OF 1863

A HEALTHY MAJOR MOSBY IN 1863

AFTER BEING WOUNDED IN THE FALL OF 1864

MOSBY IN CIVILIAN DRESS IN 1864

AS A COLONEL, NEAR WAR'S END

IN 1865, AFTER HIS MOST SERIOUS WOUNDING

AS PRIVATE CITIZEN, JUST AFTER THE WAR

A Scourge in the West

His name was Jesse James — but he was apparently no kin to the Civil War youth who would eventually become the most famous desperado in American history. Instead, this Jesse James was about 60 years of age and, in the words of one who knew him, "as good a man as resided in Ozark County." He was also the owner of a mill on the north fork of the White River near the village of Cow Skin in southwestern Missouri, and he numbered among his customers some local citizens who had remained loyal to the Union. That fact alone was sufficient to serve as James's death warrant.

One day in 1862 Jesse James, along with two men named Brown and Russell, was seized by secessionist vigilantes. What happened next was later narrated by U.S. Army Colonel Walter G. Monks, who was familiar with the event.

Having tied three lengths of rope to a long tree branch, the secessionists, wrote Monks, "rolled a big rock up to the tree where the first rope was tied to the limb, placed the noose about James' neck, stood him on the rock, rolled the rock out from under him and left him swinging, rolled the rock to the next rope, stood Brown on it, placed the noose around his neck, rolled the rock out and left Brown swinging in the air, went to the third rope, placed Russell on the rock, and just as they aimed to adjust the noose, word came that the home guards and Federals were right upon them in considerable force. They fled, leaving Russell stand-

ing upon the rock and both Brown and James dangling in the air. . . .

"The next day the wives of Brown and James, with the help of a few other women, buried them as best they could. They dug graves underneath the swinging bodies, laid bed clothing in the graves and cut them loose. The bodies fell into the coffinless graves and the earth was replaced."

Such atrocities were commonplace along the border between Missouri and Kansas, where the Civil War was but the continuation of a struggle that had been waged throughout much of the 1850s. At the heart of the violent dispute was an old question: Would Kansas enter the Union as a free state or as a slave state?

The abolitionist Kansas Free Staters were determined to keep slavery out of their new land; the proslavery men of western Missouri were every bit as determined not to be hemmed in by another free state. Legislation had failed miserably to end the dilemma: As early as 1820 the Missouri Compromise had outlawed slavery in Kansas Territory, but a later measure, the Kansas-Nebraska Act of 1854, placed the question squarely in the hands of the territory's voters — and thereby spawned a cycle of organized violence. It immediately became clear that whichever side was able to muster the most votes would have the final word in deciding the slavery issue in Kansas, and the competing factions acted at once to inundate the territory with like-minded voters. Proslavery Missourians

His disguise as an old woman uncovered, Confederate bushwhacker Cole Younger makes good his escape from Independence, Missouri, by shooting down a pair of Union sentries while clenching his horse's reins in his teeth. Younger had dressed as a woman to reconnoiter the Federally occupied town prior to an attack by Quantrill's raiders.

swept into Kansas and clustered in cities such as Lecompton. The Free Staters, joined by radical abolitionists, countered in the race to build votes by recruiting homesteaders from New England.

Inevitably violence broke out between the opposing factions, and soon rival gangs were swapping raids across the border, unleashing a cycle of looting, pillaging and murder. In 1855, more than 200 people were killed, including five farmers who were brutally murdered at Pottawatomie Creek by the rabid abolitionist John Brown. In the years directly preceding the War, the dismal succession of raids and counterraids had galvanized the fierce hatreds and had paved the way for guerrilla warfare in the border region. Even before Fort Sumter, the irregulars in this savage struggle had gained their own names: The Kansans were known as jayhawkers and

the Missourians were called bushwhackers.

Both labels had originally been meant as terms of opprobrium; both came to be worn as badges of pride. Jayhawker, a noun of obscure origin, was even converted into a verb by its practitioners, one of whom would boast in a letter to his sister: "We jayhawked. I dont suppose you know the meaning of that word that means when we are traveling through secesh country we come to the home of some leading secesh. Then we take his horses and property, burn his house, etc, or as we say, clean them out."

With the outbreak of the Civil War, veteran jayhawkers such as James H. Lane and Dr. Charles Rainsford Jennison rode out of the poisoned past and continued to carry out their depredations, now under the cloak of Federal authority. In so doing, they were engaged in bloody conflict by a new generation of bushwhackers — many of them boys unable as yet to grow beards — whose murderous campaigns were loosely sanctioned by the Confederacy.

And in their corrosive hatreds, the jayhawkers of Kansas and the bushwhackers of Missouri tore apart the border and together wrote the most brutal chapter of the American Civil War.

One of the first to enter the fray was Jim Lane, the "Grim Chieftain," a tall, bony man with a wild shock of hair and (as described by a contemporary) the "sad, dim-eyed, bad-toothed face of a harlot." A native of Indiana, Lane had been elected Lieutenant Governor of that state and then a U.S. Congressman. In Washington, as a Democrat, he cast his vote in favor of the Kansas-Nebraska Act, thereby wrecking his elective career in the free-soil state of Indiana. Partly

141

to redeem his political future, Lane moved to the abolitionist stronghold of Lawrence, Kansas, in 1855 — and almost overnight he switched sides, emerging as a prominent Republican in the Free Staters' legislature. He traveled to Washington in 1856 to petition for Kansas' admission to the Union and then returned to Kansas at the head of an army of immigrant abolitionists ready to protect the territory from the growing incursions of Border Ruffians.

At first sight, Lane cut a ludicrous figure: His habitual costume consisted of overalls, a calfskin vest and a heavy bearskin overcoat that he wore both winter and summer. Yet when Jim Lane stood up to speak, shucking his outerwear as he worked toward a crescendo, no one laughed. His voice, wrote a man who had heard him, was "a series of transitions from the broken screams of a maniac to the hoarse, rasping gutterals of a Dutch butcher in the last gasp of inebriation. And yet his extraordinary eloquence thrills like the blast of a trumpet."

Lane's demogogic tirades mesmerized increasing numbers of Kansans who had heretofore remained neutral in the border conflict. His virulent hatred of Missourians was particularly inflammatory — whether they were for or against slavery, loyal or disloyal to the Union, Missourians were all the same to Lane. "Missourians," he declared, "are wolves, snakes, devils, and damn their souls, I want to see them cast into a burning hell!"

After Kansas joined the Union as a free state on January 29, 1861, Lane was elected as one of the new state's first pair of U.S. Senators. Arriving in Washington the day after Fort Sumter, Lane quickly organized a guard to help protect the city until Federal troops could be posted and as a result won the favor of Abraham Lincoln. The President granted Lane a commission as a brigadier general in the Union Army and gave him the authority to raise troops in Kansas to protect the state from an anticipated Confederate invasion. Back in Kansas, Lane mustered three regiments, the 3rd, 4th and 5th Kansas — a motley lot of veteran jayhawkers who were subsequently described by a visitor to their camp as a "ragged, half-armed, diseased, mutinous rabble."

There was, however, a hitch: As Lane's numerous enemies in Kansas were quick to point out, he was barred by the United States Constitution from serving simultaneously as a Senator and as an officer in the U.S. Army. To Lane, the conflict mattered not a whit; retaining his Senate seat, he resigned from the U.S. Army but obtained a commission as a brigadier general in the state militia. With this title, he was able to remain in command of his jayhawkers.

In September 1861 Lane saw his chance. That month, 10,000 Confederate militiamen under Major General Sterling Price were marching north through Missouri after having defeated Federal forces in the Battle of Wilson's Creek. Lane's Brigade, as it was called, crossed the border and followed the Confederates, determined to punish the secessionist settlers who had welcomed Price's troops.

Keeping a prudent four days' march behind Price, the 1,500 jayhawkers ravaged the countryside and pillaged the settlements, more than meeting Lane's order that "everything disloyal, from a Shanghai rooster to a Durham cow, must be cleaned out." On September 22 Lane reached Osceola, one of the largest towns in western Missouri with a

Slender and youthful, Marcellus Clark was often mistaken for a woman by the victims of his raids, despite the twin revolvers he wore and the stiletto (*above*) he carried disguised as a cane.

The Saga of a Raider Called Sue

Readers of the Louisville *Courier* in 1864 were intrigued to learn that the band of Confederate guerrillas roaming Kentucky was led by a woman. Her name, the paper said, was Sue Mundy.

Actually, Sue Mundy was a young man, small and long-haired, named Marcellus Clark, the scion of a distinguished family. The newspaper had brazenly invented his female persona — even borrowing the name of a notorious local madam — to embarrass the Federal army commander in Louisville, with whom it was feuding.

The hoax worked, and by early 1865 the capture of Sue Mundy's gang had become an urgent priority, especially after well-publicized accounts related that she had joined forces with William Quantrill's raiders. A few weeks before the War's end, a troop of Wisconsin cavalry captured Clark in a Kentucky barn. He demanded to be treated as a prisoner of war. But because of "Sue Mundy's" infamous celebrity, he was hanged as a criminal instead.

population of 2,500. His discovery of military supplies in a warehouse gave Lane all the excuse he needed to raze and plunder the town. His men burned all but three buildings; robbed the banks, stores and homes of private citizens; shot nine civilians who may or may not have been disloyal to the Union; and departed for Lawrence — at least 300 of the brigade so drunk that they had to ride in wagons they had stolen. With them went 350 horses and mules, along with 200 newly liberated slaves. As for Jim Lane, his personal share of the loot was a handsome carriage, a piano and a large number of silk dresses for his female acquaintances.

Compared with the magnitude of later outrages, the sacking of Osceola was a minor affair. Yet it was not soon forgotten by the Missouri bushwhackers. Three years later a gang of them would massacre the inhabitants of a Kansas town while screaming a battle cry

that consisted of a single word — "Osceola!"

Osceola was the high-water mark of Jim Lane's career as a jayhawker. By November, his troops had been ordered to duty at Fort Scott, in southeastern Kansas. Thereafter, even while he retained his firm political control of the war against the bushwhackers, Lane began gradually to withdraw from personal participation in jayhawking raids. And his title as one of the most notorious of the active jayhawkers fell naturally to a dapper medical man who wore the self-satisfied look of a fox that had just paid a profitable call on the henhouse.

Like Lane, Charles R. Jennison was a relative newcomer to the Kansas-Missouri border: Born in upstate New York, he moved at the age of 12 to Wisconsin, where he studied medicine and briefly practiced as a doctor before moving on to Kansas and settling in

1858 in Mound City, only a few miles from the Missouri line. Unlike the gangling "Grim Chieftain," however, Doc Jennison was a tiny man. One acquaintance remarked that he was barely visible above his high-top boots; to give the illusion of height, he habitually wore a tall, Cossack-type fur cap. And in direct contrast to the cynical Jim Lane, Jennison's abolitionist sentiments came not as a matter of opportunism but out of passionate conviction.

Almost from the day he arrived, Jennison was a leading citizen of Mound City. Doctors, of course, were in short supply on the frontier, and Jennison's services were badly needed. Beyond that, he displayed a strong sense of civic pride: When the nearby village of Paris contested Mound City for the honor of being the county seat, Jennison rounded up a bunch of locals, laid his hands on a howitzer, went over to Paris and forcibly removed all the county records. That put an end to the argument.

Jennison was also a shrewd businessman. On nearby Creek and Cherokee Indian reservations, cattle were being devoured by packs of ravening wolves. Calling upon his medical knowledge, Jennison demonstrated to the Indians how to get rid of the beasts by leaving them meat poisoned with strychnine. Then, at what someone described as "an enormous price," he sold the Indians a barrel, mislabeled "strychnine," that was, in fact, filled with flour.

For all his sidelines, Jennison's first love was abolition. He rode for a time with James Montgomery, one of the pioneering jayhawkers, then broke away to form a vigilante committee that soon became notorious for its accomplishments at horse thievery, pillage and the dispensing of justice at the end of a noose. In the autumn of 1860 Jennison and his men raided the nearby village of Trading Post and arrested all residents suspected of favoring slavery. Among those citizens held was a wretch named Russell Hinds, who eked out his living by capturing and returning runaway slaves to Missourians at five dollars a head.

Hinds was tried on the spot by a jury of jayhawkers, found guilty and hanged. By way of explanation, Jennison later issued a statement to newspapers. "It was never our intention," he wrote, "to meddle with anyone's political views unless he shall have been engaged in manhunting, or has by the commission of some high crime forfeited the right to live among us."

During the first months of the War, Jennison's raiders acquired the status of a Kansas militia company and began calling themselves the Mound City Sharp's Rifle Guards. Under that name — and occasionally joining forces with Jim Lane's roughnecks — they embarked on a series of hit-and-run raids that was highlighted in July 1861 by a foray against the Missouri hamlet of Morristown. There they stole everything in sight and shot dead a man who objected to being robbed of his mule. On the next day, the jayhawkers divided among themselves loot worth $2,000 — just about everything of value that Morristown had possessed.

By late summer, Jennison's activities had reached such a fever pitch that Kansas Governor Charles Robinson, a moderate and a bitter political enemy to Jim Lane, feared that the little doctor would provoke a full-scale retaliatory attack by Missourians against Kansas. As a solution, Robinson shrewdly urged Federal authorities to give Jennison a colonel's commission and accept

Seen here in a damaged photograph, Kansas Senator James H. Lane was described by his archenemy, the bushwhacker William Quantrill, as "the chief of all the Jayhawkers and the worst man that was ever born into this world." Later, when asked on his deathbed what he might have done with Lane had he captured him, Quantrill replied forthrightly: "I would have burned him at the stake."

his jayhawkers into the Union cavalry. This move would curb Jennison and his men by placing them under military discipline; and as the cagey Robinson knew full well, it would at the same time isolate one of Lane's most important allies.

So it happened that on October 28, 1861, at Fort Leavenworth, Colonel Charles R. Jennison presided over the ceremony that mustered in the Mound City Sharp's Rifle Guard as the 7th Kansas Volunteer Cavalry Regiment — soon to be known throughout the border country as Jennison's Jayhawkers. Unfortunately for the dignity of the occasion, the regiment's colonel knew nothing about military commands, and his attempt to drill the men produced utter confusion — whereupon Jennison jauntily rode off to nearby Squiresville to indulge in his favorite pastime of draw poker.

As matters evolved, Governor Robinson's strategy for restraining Jennison's Jayhawkers was no more than a forlorn hope. Within days after it was formally organized, the 7th Kansas was ordered to Kansas City, Missouri, whence it was assigned to escort a train of 500 ox-drawn government supply wagons to Sedalia, Missouri. This was routine duty, and not at all to the jayhawkers' liking. And so, dire warnings were issued: "Woe be to that country if these transports are molested," cried Lieutenant Colonel Daniel Anthony, Jennison's second-in-command; and then the 7th Kansas sent the wagons off unescorted and turned its attention to more profitable affairs.

On November 14, Jennison's men, along with those of Lane, fresh from Osceola, struck at Independence, Missouri, about 10 miles from Kansas City. There they rounded up the townsmen, ordered a local citizen to separate all the secessionists and forced them to take loyalty oaths. Then the jayhawkers plundered the town.

Meanwhile, on November 18 the wagon train to Sedalia had been held up and robbed by Missouri guerrillas. In reprisal, the 7th Kansas sacked and burned the town of Pleasant Hill, southwest of Kansas City — decades later, villagers would still recall the occasion as "Jennison's Day."

As the year neared its end, Jennison's Jayhawkers rode from their Kansas City base to the border town of West Point, Missouri, expressly, as Brigadier General James W. Denver put it, to "protect the frontier of Kansas from incursions of the rebel bands now in that neighborhood." On the way, recalled one Kansan, they scorched the Missouri side of the border: "Every house along our line of march but one was burned, and off on our left flank for miles, columns of smoke from burning houses and barns could be seen."

For the next two months, the 7th Kansas enjoyed what one of them called "the strenuous life." In jayhawker terms, that meant laying waste to the countryside and pillaging hamlets. Arriving at Harrisonville, Jennison's Jayhawkers discovered that another gang of marauding Unionists had got there ahead of them and stripped the town of everything but the Bibles in a depository of the American Bible Society. Undaunted, the Kansans stole the Bibles.

By now, however, Doc Jennison's rule of ruin was nearing its end. Across the state in St. Louis, Major General Henry W. Halleck had taken command of the Department of the West, which included all the Federal forces in Missouri. Halleck was an officer who went by the book, and he abhorred the

jayhawkers' undisciplined behavior. "They are," he wrote to General George B. McClellan in December of 1861, "no better than a band of robbers."

Moreover, Halleck was alarmed by the response of western Missourians to Jennison's depredations. At the start of the War, the region had been more or less equally divided among secessionists, Unionists and those who declined to take sides. Now, in the anger aroused by the jayhawker raids, more and more people, including a great many who had previously favored the Union, were switching their allegiance to the Confedera-

The fiercest jayhawker, Colonel Charles Jennison (*right*), organized and led the 7th Kansas Cavalry, the notorious regiment whose savage raids into Missouri (*below*) were monuments to murder and rapine. Jennison boasted that Missouri mothers could hush their children to sleep with the mere mention of his name.

cy. "The conduct of these forces," Halleck continued, "has done more for the enemy in this state than could have been accomplished by 20,000 of his own army. These men disgrace the name and uniform of American soldiers and are driving good Union men into the ranks of the secession army." If that trend kept up, Halleck added, the state of Missouri would soon be "as Confederate as eastern Virginia."

In January of 1862 the clamor against jayhawking outrages had risen to a crescendo, and Halleck made his move. The 7th Kansas was ordered out of Missouri and to Humboldt, Kansas, a town far enough from the border to make jayhawking impractical. Then in March the regiment was sent to Lawrence and ordered to prepare for trans-

fer to the deserts of New Mexico for duty in Indian country. The 7th Kansas would be about 1,000 miles from Henry Halleck — and none too far at that.

Fighting Mescalero Apaches in New Mexico was by no means what Doc Jennison had had in mind when he took up arms, and on April 11 he tendered his Army resignation — which was accepted with almost indecent haste. In his farewell speech to his troops, Jennison railed against his detractors, and soon he was arrested on vague charges that included his use of "contemptuous and disrespectful language" toward, among others, General Halleck. Released after a few days, Jennison flourished for a while as a martyr to the cause of Radical Republicans and eventually won reinstatement as a Union colonel. But his days as the scourge of the Missouri-Kansas border were essentially over.

As for Jennison's Jayhawkers, they were sent not to New Mexico but to Corinth, Mississippi, where their chronic indiscipline became a source of endless distress to a succession of Union commanders.

Back in Missouri, droves of men had banded together in response to the jayhawker raids; their motives were many: hatred, revenge, or merely a simple craving for adventure. In action, these men were to spawn a wave of terror in which few border settlers could remain neutral. Their most infamous leader was, in the words of a Union soldier sent to hunt him, "a notorious raskal by the name of Quantral."

His actual name was William Clarke Quantrill, and by any standard he was an enigma — a Yankee who murdered for the South, a Kansas jayhawker who betrayed his com-

William Quantrill, a gambler, thief and prewar jayhawker, autographed this photograph of himself, taken in Lawrence, Kansas, in 1860. Three years later, having changed allegiance, he would return to ravage Lawrence at the head of a ruthless bushwhacker horde. Shown above is one of Quantrill's Colt Army six-shooters — a weapon he could fire with deadly accuracy while riding at a gallop.

rades to become a Missouri bushwhacker.

The oldest of 12 children born to an Ohio schoolteacher, Quantrill himself was a teacher at the age of 16. Four years later he wandered westward and worked his way as far as Utah before turning back and taking up residence — under the assumed name of Charley Hart — in Lawrence, Kansas, about 40 miles from the Missouri line. Before long he was running with local toughs who jayhawked across the border for pleasure and stole horses — including those of their neighbors — for profit. The first enterprise was permissible but the second was not, and Quantrill soon found himself a very short step ahead of the law. Realizing that he had more than worn out his welcome, Quantrill determined to quit Kansas — and the manner of departure that he chose revealed in him a strain of ruthlessness.

In December 1860 Quantrill accompanied five young Quaker abolitionists on a mission to liberate the 26 slaves of a prosperous Missouri farmer named Morgan Walker; so confident of success were the jayhawkers that they had even brought along a wagon to transport Walker's slaves back to Kansas and freedom. When the Kansans neared the farm, Quantrill rode ahead of the others on the pretense of reconnoitering. Instead, he seized the opportunity to inform Walker's family of the imminent raid — and when the unsuspecting Quakers arrived, they rode straight into a shotgun ambush. Three of the abolitionists were killed.

Quantrill had a ready lie to excuse his betrayal: The Quakers, he said, had been members of a jayhawker gang that had murdered his older brother, and he had arranged their deaths as a matter of vengeance. This, of course, was something that the Missourians could admire, and Quantrill's status as an avenging angel earned him instant admission into Missouri's bushwhacking society. By December 1861, after a year of raiding with other marauders, Quantrill had organized his own band of bushwhackers. Originally comprising 10 youths, it included an itinerant young stonemason named George Todd, who was destined one day to make even Quantrill cringe in terror.

Now 24, William Quantrill was of average height — about five feet nine inches tall — and slight of build, with a pallid complexion and a mustache that made him appear as if he would be more comfortable on a riverboat with a deck of cards in his hands than a pair of over-size revolvers. Only the heavily hooded eyes — cold, pale and blue — gave any indication of the natural killer who resided within.

There was nothing subtle about Quantrill's tactics; he relied almost entirely on sudden, headlong charges at the enemy, secure in the knowledge that his men possessed firepower superior to that of their victims. Each of his bushwhackers carried four or five Colt revolvers either on his person or within handy reach on his saddle. Against such weaponry, even the Union cavalry was outmatched, since most troopers at that stage of the War were armed with muskets or muzzle-loading carbines.

Thus, in raid after raid, Quantrill established himself as the terror of the Missouri-Kansas border country. On March 22, 1862, for example, 100 of his gang burned a bridge over the Blue River near Kansas City and murdered the tollkeeper while his little boy watched; they also beat a Federal guard and then shot him dead — in direct reprisal, it was said, for an order issued by General Halleck that captured bushwhackers should be hanged "as robbers and murderers."

All through the summer of 1862 Quantrill's band robbed Union mails, ambushed Federal patrols and attacked boats on the Missouri River. In September they fell on Olathe, Kansas, burning the newspaper office and killing three civilians while Quan-

trill swaggered about the town, informing old Kansas acquaintances that he should now be addressed as captain. In fact, he had apparently received a Confederate captain's commission that had been authorized by Major General Thomas Hindman, then the commander of the Trans-Mississippi District. (Thereafter, Quantrill simply promoted himself, ending his career as a colonel.)

By the autumn of 1862, Quantrill's gang numbered 150 men, and on October 17 they galloped toward Shawneetown, Kansas, bent on destruction. Approaching the town, they encountered a Federal supply train, encircled it and, howling like prairie Indians, killed 15 drivers and members of the Union escort. Then they plundered Shawneetown, shooting down 10 men and burning the village to the ground.

In November 1862, anticipating a scarcity of food over the winter, Quantrill and his bushwhackers rode south to Confederate-held Arkansas, where General Sterling Price's army could provide them with rations. It was not until May of the following year that Federal authorities on the Missouri border learned some highly unwelcome news: Quantrill was back.

He took up where he had left off, and before long his rampages had become so commonplace that the Kansas City *Journal of Commerce* stated as a matter of simple fact, "Quantrill & Co. do rule in this section of the state."

At that time, Union forces in the region had recently been reorganized, and the commander of the so-called District of the Border was a general who clearly meant business. Brigadier General Thomas Ewing Jr., a brother-in-law to William Tecumseh Sherman, determined that he would strike at the

Quantrill's Bloody Bushwhackers

LITTLE ARCHIE CLEMENT

JOHN JARRETTE

COLE AND JIM YOUNGER

FRANK JAMES

BLOODY BILL ANDERSON

GEORGE MADDOX

GEORGE TODD

bushwhackers where they were most vulnerable — that is, through the women who gave them food and shelter (and lovingly stitched designs on the "guerrilla shirts" that had come to distinguish them). During the summer, Ewing rounded up mothers, wives, sisters and sweethearts of some of the more notorious bushwhackers and clapped them into confinement.

Soon a tragedy occurred that would have dire consequences. About a dozen of the women were being held on the second floor of a three-story Kansas City building so dilapidated that makeshift rafters were required to shore up its roof and ceilings. On August 14 the building collapsed, killing five of the women and seriously injuring several others. Among those crushed to death was a girl named Josephine Anderson; her 16-year-old sister Mary was badly hurt. Their brother William was already making a name for himself as one of the more vicious of Quantrill's gang, and when he heard of the tragedy his frail hold on sanity snapped. Known as Bloody Bill Anderson, the maniacal man would henceforth ride into battle sobbing and frothing at the mouth.

The bushwhackers were convinced that General Ewing had deliberately caused the accident by undermining the building. And four days later he fueled their outrage by issuing his General Order No. 10, which required that "the wives and children of known guerrillas move out of this district and out of the State of Missouri forthwith."

By a coincidence of timing, the order played right into the hands of Quantrill. At the moment it was issued, he was presiding over a gathering of bushwhackers in the Blackwater Creek country of western Missouri. For some time now, Quantrill had been planning his boldest raid to date — against the abolitionist town of Lawrence, Kansas. Quantrill had ample cause for harboring a grudge against Lawrence: Not only was it the town from which he had been driven as an outlaw, but it was the home of the jayhawker Jim Lane. In preparation for the expedition, Quantrill had gone so far as to send spies to Lawrence, where they noted the prominent abolitionists and jotted those names on a death list.

Yet despite Quantrill's argument that Lawrence was the place where the bushwhackers could "get more revenge and more money than anywhere else," some of his raiders had been reluctant, insisting that the town was too strongly defended. But such doubts were overwhelmed by the frenzy of rage that followed the announcement of Ewing's General Order No. 10, coming as it did on top of the Kansas City disaster. "We could stand no more," cried one of the bushwhackers — and on August 19, 1863, Quantrill, at the head of 300 men, started out for the Kansas town that would become forever associated with his name.

Along the way, the Missourians picked up 150 more men. Crossing the Kansas border, they were spotted by a Federal officer, who alerted his district headquarters in Kansas City but unaccountably failed to send warnings to the Federal outposts that lay in the bushwhackers' line of march. During the journey, the bushwhackers forced at least 10 Kansas farmers into service as local guides and then, when their usefulness was done, gunned them down where they stood. At one point, the invading riders stopped at a farmhouse where the surly stonemason, George Todd, recognized a man who had once caused him trouble with the law in Kansas

City. Without any ado, Todd beat the man to death with the butt of a musket.

Steadily, in column of fours beneath a moonless sky, the bushwhackers progressed across the Kansas plains, as one rider said, "like a monstrous snake, creeping upon its prey." At dawn on August 21 they paused on a hill just short of their destination. Even then, some of the men wanted to turn back; the townsfolk of Lawrence, they insisted, must surely have been warned by now of their approach. "You can do as you please," said Quantrill. "I am going into Lawrence." Then, drawing one of the four revolvers he carried in his belt, he spurred his horse and shouted: "Charge!"

Into the town and down its streets they thundered, Quantrill exhorting his men with shouts of "Kill! Kill! Lawrence must be cleansed, and the only way to cleanse it is to kill! Kill!" The first victim to be shot down was a preacher named Snyder, who toppled under the cow he had been milking in his yard. Near the center of town, a detachment of 22 Union Army recruits was encamped; the mounted bushwhackers, yelling their vengeful cry "Osceola!" surged over the drowsy soldiers, shooting some and trampling others beneath the pounding hoofs of their horses. In all, 17 Federals were slaughtered; the other five escaped. Then, while Quantrill ate a hearty breakfast in a Lawrence hotel, the bushwhackers carried out his orders to "kill every man big enough to carry a gun." Most were shot in cold blood as they stood in their doorways; some were burned to death when a torch was put to buildings in which they were hiding; the town's mayor was suffocated by smoke in the bottom of a well where he had sought safety.

For four hours the killing continued. Finally, about 9 a.m., the bushwhackers got word that Union troops were approaching, so they headed at a gallop back to Missouri — leaving behind them a ruined town where dozens of fires licked at the buildings and where the bodies of at least 150 men lay strewn about. (Women, by Quantrill's order, had been spared, although several were robbed of their wedding rings.) Among the Kansans who survived — to Quantrill's great chagrin — was Jim Lane, whom the bushwhackers had meant to take alive and carry back to Missouri for execution, either by public hanging or by burning at the stake. Instead, Lane, awakened from his slumbers, had leaped from bed, cagily removed a metal nameplate from his house (which was soon burned) and, in his nightshirt, scurried into hiding in a nearby cornfield.

Throughout that terrible morning, the bushwhackers suffered only one casualty. On their departure, a former Baptist preacher named Larkin Skaggs had been left behind, too drunk to ride. Skaggs was shot to death by a local Indian. His body was dragged through the streets behind a horse, then ripped apart by the enraged survivors of the Lawrence massacre.

In grim aftermath, on August 23, a Sunday, someone mistook the smoke from a trash fire for a signal that the bushwhackers were returning to Lawrence. "Quantrill is coming! Quantrill is coming!" went the horrified cry — and, according to one account, "most of the men and all of the women and children fled and spent the entire night in a field in the rain."

As a direct result of the bloodbath at Lawrence, General Ewing on August 25 instituted one of the most repressive measures ever

inflicted on an American civilian population. Under his General Order No. 11, nearly all the inhabitants of three Missouri border counties and half of another, were given 15 days in which to vacate their homes and remove all their belongings from the area. Even those citizens who could offer positive proof of their loyalty to the Union were required to move to the shelter of Federal military posts or to the interior of Kansas.

For two sorrowful weeks, the evacuation went on, made all the worse by jayhawkers who, despite Ewing's continued attempts to restrain them, swarmed across the border and slashed at the heels of the departing Missourians, robbing many of their meager possessions and burning their abandoned homes. Even a Union officer, Colonel Bazel Lazear, was moved to pity: "It is heart sickening to see what I have seen since I have been back here," he wrote. "A desolated country and men & women and children, some of them almost naked. Some on foot and some in old wagons. Oh God." The land that the little caravans left behind was studded with chimneys still standing amid the smoldering ruins of what had once been homes; the region would be known for many years as the Burnt District.

The bushwhackers who had caused the evacuation were scarcely bothered. Easily avoiding both Union troops and roving jayhawkers, they lived off the smoked hams, the slabs of bacon and the maverick cattle left behind by the departing Missourians and overlooked by the Kansas marauders. Quantrill himself holed up near Blue Springs, Missouri, and dallied away the time in the company of 16-year-old Kate King, who borrowed her lover's middle name and was now called Kate Clarke.

In late September, when Quantrill's gang

In the early-morning light of August 21, 1863, Quantrill's pro-Confederate raiders run rampant through the streets of Lawrence, Kansas — long an abolitionist bastion. Some of the raiders carried lists of men slated for execution. Others murdered at random: One 12-year-old boy, wearing a suit made for him by his mother out of a Union soldier's uniform, was chased down by a bushwhacker and shot in the head.

was approaching from the north — a far more inviting target than the angry and obstinate Federals in the fort. Deploying 250 bushwhackers in line of battle, Quantrill waited for the wagons to draw closer.

On they came, escorted by about 100 troopers of the 3rd Wisconsin and 14th Kansas Cavalry and, unbeknownst to Quantrill, accompanied by none other than Major General James G. Blunt, commander of the Union's District of the Frontier. A harddrinking, hard-fighting abolitionist who owed his job to the auspices of Jim Lane, Blunt ranked nearly as high as his sponsor on the list of Unionists the bushwhackers would like to see dead.

Riding in a buggy, Blunt peered ahead and saw the bushwhackers ready to meet him. Since most of them wore blue uniforms taken in the past from Union dead, Blunt assumed that these riders were from the fort at Baxter Springs — either a detachment out drilling or an honor guard sent to greet him. Into the trap the Federals rode. At a range of about 60 yards, Quantrill's men loosed a murderous volley that broke the ranks of Blunt's escort. Seeing confusion and panic, the bushwhackers then charged. Within minutes, the affair was decided. Quantrill's men looted and burned the wagons. Many of the Federals surrendered, only to be shot down where they stood. One of the few who escaped was General Blunt, who had jumped from his buggy during the fray and onto the back of a swift horse.

The Union soldiers who later arrived on the scene found, according to Colonel Charles Blair, "a fearful sight: some 85 bodies nearly all shot through the head, most shot from 5 to 7 times each, horribly mangled, charred and blackened by fire." A

did leave Missouri, it was not because it had been forced from the state but rather because the bushwhackers were once more ready to take up winter quarters, this time in Texas. Along the way, their depredations would continue.

Early in October, Quantrill and 400 men crossed into Kansas and headed south. On October 6, scouts reported that Federal troops had built a small earth-and-log fort at Baxter Springs, dead ahead in the bushwhacker's path. Sensing an easy kill, Quantrill ordered his advance guard to attack the fort; it did, but it was beaten back by the 150-man Union garrison.

Meanwhile, Quantrill was still outside town with the rest of his men when word came that a 10-wagon Union supply train

A distraught family reacts to the murder of a kinsman who resisted evacuation in the wake of General Thomas Ewing's Order No. 11, which forced virtually all those living in western Missouri border counties to leave their homes in August 1863. Artist George Caleb Bingham, a staunch Unionist but a bitter critic of the order, painted this imagined scene with the stated purpose of discrediting Ewing, who is shown looking on from his bay horse.

drummer boy, according to another officer, had been shot and thrown senseless under a burning wagon where he regained consciousness and "crawled a distance of 30 yards, marking the course by bits of burning clothes and scorched grass" before he died.

Late in October, Quantrill's band crossed the Red River and settled down for the winter in Texas. The men immediately embarked on a prolonged drinking spree. No one in authority knew quite what to do about them. In fact, Confederate officials were growing increasingly uneasy about Quantrill and his men. Missouri Governor Tom Reynolds, a secessionist, had already compared the gang to "an elephant won in a raffle." Confederate Army commanders had begun to question whether Quantrill was as dedicated to the Confederate cause as he was addicted to blood lust and booty. And, to a man, the Confederate Army officers abhorred Quantrill's brutal methods of fighting. Brigadier General Henry McCulloch, on duty in Texas, wrote that "Quantrill's mode of warfare, from all I can learn, is but little if not all removed from that of the wildest savage. If he is an officer his conduct should be officially noticed, and if not his conduct should be officially disavowed."

For all the concern, however, no Confederate authority moved to discipline Quantrill. At the most, he did receive some pressure to enter the Confederate Army, which he ignored. Among those who urged him to do so was Governor Reynolds, who in a letter gave Quantrill a reason to quit his current course: "The history of every guerrilla chief has been the same. He either becomes the slave of his men, or if he attempts to control them, some officer or private rises up, disputes his authority, gains the men, and puts him down."

Reynolds' warning proved to be prophetic. During the idle months in Texas, Quantrill lost control of his command. His obvious loss of esteem among Army regulars had disillusioned many of his followers; others chafed at inequities in the division of the spoils; and still others, apparently, were sickened by the bloody excesses of the past. At any rate, the gang broke into factions— both George Todd and Bill Anderson had their own followers— and quarreled bitterly. At one point, Quantrill and Todd actually exchanged fire; the fight was stopped by some of the men before any blood was shed, but the acrimony remained.

For the time being, however, Anderson posed a more urgent threat to Quantrill's leadership. During the winter, he had taken residence in Sherman with a saloon girl named Bush Smith, and while he was enjoying her company, his followers ran wild. Confederate authorities understandably held Quantrill accountable. Finally, in a belated attempt to impose discipline, Quantrill ordered one of Anderson's men shot as a thief; at that, the psychotic Anderson burst into a rage, declared that he would not remain with "such a damn outfit" and, with about 20 bushwhackers, rode off toward Bonham, Texas.

Quantrill pursued, and for several days the rival gangs engaged in running gunfights across the Texas plains. The result was a stalemate, and a troubled peace settled on the hostile camps until, in the spring of 1864, Quantrill and Anderson led their men by separate routes back to Missouri.

There, a showdown between Quantrill and Todd occurred almost immediately.

While they were playing cards in a farmhouse, Quantrill accused Todd of cheating. Todd pulled a gun on Quantrill, and the guerrilla leader decided not to press the issue. William Quantrill walked out of the room — and, as an effective leader, out of the Missouri-Kansas border wars.

Todd now assumed leadership of Quantrill's followers, while Bloody Bill Anderson remained on his own. Hiding out in the rugged Sni-a-Bar country east of Kansas City, Todd repeatedly made strikes against Union personnel and property. Yet he got the worst of encounters with the crack 2nd Colorado Cavalry Regiment, which had been brought in to deal with the bushwhackers. During a 20-day period in July, General Egbert Brown, commander of Missouri's Central District, sent out more than 100 patrols that rode over 10,000 miles while losing 42 men and killing about 100 bushwhackers.

During that same summer of 1864, Bloody Bill Anderson covered himself with gruesome glory. On July 24, with 100 riders, Anderson waylaid a Union detachment near his

Members of an ill-fated military band congregate near Union General James Blunt's Kansas headquarters. The musicians would be with Blunt at Baxter Springs, Kansas, on October 6, 1863, when Quantrill's raiders attacked their outnumbered party; all 14 of these bandsmen were slain.

Major General James G. Blunt, commander of the Union's District of the Frontier at the time of the Baxter Springs assault, was an abolitionist who associated with John Brown before the War. Blunt escaped capture; his barber was taken by Quantrill's men to Texas to trim their hair.

northern Missouri hometown of Huntsville. Although most of the Federals escaped, two were killed — and then scalped by Little Archie Clement, an 18-year-old murderer who habitually wore a sadistic smirk. Before they left, the bushwhackers attached to one of the bodies a note signed by Bill Anderson: "You come to hunt bush whackers. Now you are skelpt. Clemyent skelpt you."

A month later, near Rocheport, Missouri, Anderson ambushed and overran a patrol of the 4th Missouri Cavalry detailed to chase the guerrillas, killing seven soldiers — of whom four were found scalped and three others found with their throats slit.

Throughout the atrocities, Bloody Bill, who was by no means as illiterate as the note that he had left on the corpse made him out to be, used Missouri newspapers to engage in a war of words. In a letter to one editor, he issued a warning to the citizens of Missouri: "If you proclaim to be in arms against the guerrillas I will kill you. I will hunt you down like wolves and murder you. You

cannot escape." In another letter, he taunted a Union colonel about the marksmanship of Federal troops: "They are such poor shots it is strange you don't have them practice more. Send them out and I will train them for you."

Late in September, Anderson suffered one of his few setbacks — and it unloosed all the demons that lay within him. Joining forces with Todd's gang, Anderson launched an assault against 30 men of the state militia's 9th Cavalry, who were defending a fortified brick courthouse and a nearby blockhouse at Fayette, Missouri. Time and again, Anderson led headlong charges against the buildings; time and again he was repulsed. "It was like charging a stone wall only this stone wall belched lead," recalled a bushwhacker named Frank James (who, along with his younger brother Jesse, would become an outlaw after the War). Then he added: "The worst scared I ever was during the war was in the Fayette fight."

In that action, the bushwhackers lost 13 dead and 30 wounded. A few days later, however, Bloody Bill Anderson got an opportunity for revenge.

On the evening of September 26, 1864, the men under Anderson and Todd camped together on a farm near the tiny Missouri railroad town of Centralia. Early the next morning, apparently eager to read accounts of his activities, Anderson ordered 30 of his men into their saddles; leaving Todd's people behind, they rode into Centralia to fetch St. Louis newspapers.

At the Centralia depot, a few of the men found a barrel of whiskey, along with a crate of boots. Pouring the liquor into the boots, they forced some of the townspeople to drink. At the same time, the bushwhackers downed huge gulps of whiskey, and they were soon reeling drunk. For the next three hours they amused themselves by looting the little town and setting fire to the depot. Just as they were preparing to depart, Anderson stopped them with a gleeful shout: "Look out, boys! A train is coming! Let's stop it! Block the track!"

By the time the westbound train rolled into the smoking station, the bushwhackers had blocked the track with ties. Ordered out of the train, the 125 passengers — including at least 25 uniformed but unarmed Federal soldiers going home on leave — found themselves in the midst of a screaming, dancing mob of drunken bushwhackers.

Dividing the passengers into two groups — one of civilians and the other of soldiers — Anderson ordered the Army men to strip, and in a shrill, mad voice, he informed them of their fate: "You are all to be killed and sent to hell." Naked and trembling, the soldiers were lined up along the station platform. Turning to Little Archie Clement, Anderson told him to "muster out" the helpless Federals. Grinning happily, Clement started to shoot. Other bushwhackers joined in, and by the time they had finished, 22 of the soldiers lay dead.

Shouting, laughing, drinking and still shooting, the bushwhackers finally rode out of town and returned to camp, where they boasted of their exploits to Todd's men. Four hours after Anderson's departure, a 150-man Union detail of the 39th Missouri Infantry, commanded by Major A.V.E. Johnston, rode into Centralia; they had been following the bushwhackers' trail and had seen a column of smoke rising from the town. Johnston's soldiers were green recruits, and doubtless he was greatly relieved

Bloody Bill Anderson still clutches his Colt revolver in a death portrait taken after he was slain by Federal militiamen near Richmond, Missouri, on October 26, 1864. Anderson's embroidered shirt and trimmed hat were not his only flourishes: He also adorned his horse's bridle with the scalps of his victims.

to learn that Anderson had left with only 30 men. Johnston stationed 35 of his soldiers in the town and went after the guerrillas with the bulk of his command.

The soldiers' approach was seen by the bushwhackers, who now numbered several hundred. The guerrillas quickly formed a long, crescent-shaped line out of sight behind a gentle rise. To lure the Federals on, Anderson sent out 10 men under Little Archie Clement, who played his part to perfection. Approaching almost to within firing range of the Union column, Clement and his men suddenly wheeled their horses and fled. Johnston's men pounded after them — and entered the jaws of the trap.

Coming over the rise, Major Johnston saw the bushwhackers in line at the foot of the slope; realizing that he had led his inexperienced men into an ambush, he ordered them to dismount and form a line of battle. "God help 'em," shouted one of Todd's bushwhackers. "The fools are going to fight us on foot." But there was no help to be had on that September day. "Charge!" cried Anderson, and he led the bushwhackers as they roared up the hill.

Johnston's troopers managed to get in only one volley from their single-shot Enfield muskets. Then, with the bushwhackers upon them from all sides, they dropped their weapons, turned in panic, fled — and died. By the time the firing faded away, Union bodies lay so thick on the field that one of the bushwhackers capered saying, "I cannot count 'em good unless I step on 'em." When he had finished, the count stood at nearly 115. Among those killed was Major Johnston, shot by a revolver in the hands of 17-year-old Jesse James.

Two days later, Brigadier General Clinton Fisk, the district commander, reported in sickening detail what his soldiers had found when they arrived, too late, at the scene of the massacre. Some of Johnston's men, he wrote, "were shot through the head, then scalped, bayonets thrust through them, ears and noses cut off, and privates torn off and thrust in the mouths of the dying."

At the time of the Centralia massacre, the bushwhackers seemed to be as deadly as ever. It appeared that Bill Anderson and George Todd would be committing their butcheries for a long time to come.

And then, suddenly, they were gone.

On October 21, less than a month after Centralia, Todd was watching his men fight jayhawkers near Independence when a sniper's bullet crashed into his neck. He died an hour later, suffocating in his own blood.

Just five days later, Bloody Bill Anderson and about 70 of his bushwhackers were cornered by Union militiamen in northwestern Missouri. Although greatly outnumbered, Anderson did as he had always done — he charged. Anderson broke through the Union line and kept going. But then, his revolvers still smoking, he raised his arms, fell backward off his horse, and died with two bullets in the back of his head.

Now the Civil War was over, the bugles silenced, the soldiers returning to their homes. Many of the guerrillas, too, were able to return to peaceable lives after the War. But others could not change their lawless ways, and they applied the tactics they had learned as guerrillas to new livelihoods as highwaymen and bank robbers.

Todd and Anderson were not the only ones who came to a violent end. During the months after his exile from the Missouri gangs, William Clarke Quantrill had found consolation in the arms of Kate Clarke. Then, toward the end of 1864, he had grown restless and, gathering up a handful of men, had gone to Kentucky. There, on May 10, 1865, nearly a month after the War had ended, he was surprised and shot by Union soldiers. Before he died, Quantrill was baptized as a Roman Catholic.

And finally, on July 1, 1865, James H. Lane, for reasons understood only in the dark crypts of his mind, took out a revolver and fired what was perhaps the last shot of the jayhawker-bushwhacker war — into his own mouth.

Fantastic Weapons to End the War

In August of 1862 a mechanic from Jonesville, Michigan, named C. G. Birbeck wrote to Secretary of War Edwin M. Stanton to call attention to what he believed would be an essential ingredient in the Union's ultimate victory. That ingredient, wrote Birbeck, was cayenne pepper. He went on to suggest that the simple expedient of loading Union artillery shells with the stuff would wreak havoc on the Confederates: Clouds of pepper dust would descend on their ranks like "a destroying angel," and incapacitate them with fits of sneezing. History does not record Secretary Stanton's reaction to the idea, but Birbeck's proposition was certainly not the only outlandish notion to reach him during the war years.

Thousands of aspiring inventors bombarded Washington with plans for bold new weapons that they hoped would bring about a swifter end to the fighting. Not all of these inventions were hopelessly farfetched. The persistent attempts to develop a rapid-firing weapon, for instance, led eventually to the highly successful Gatling gun (page 169), although the final version was not adopted by the War Department until after the War. Other suggestions, though ingenious, proved beyond the technological capabilities of the time. Such was the case with the tanklike land monitor (page 171), which looked rather like a turtle on wheels.

In Washington, where the War Department had trouble enough arming its forces with conventional weapons, such flights of fancy were generally regarded as ludicrous. Only a few of the designs shown on these pages were ever built and tested, and fewer still saw battle. Most of the plans — despite the good intentions of the inventors — went back to the drawing board.

In this breathless handbill, a Mr. Hebert claims to have invented a cannon capable of firing 12 shots in half a minute. Such a weapon, had it really existed, would have dramatically altered the course of the War.

GREAT INVENTION

MR. HEBERT

A Mechanic, having spent a great deal of time to construct a

CANNON!

Would inform the citizens of this place that it is complete. The cannon will shoot

TWELVE SHOTS IN A HALF A MINUTE!

If loaded beforehand, or if loaded while being discharged

Twelve Shots a Minute!

Without heating, hundreds having been given up for the reason that it would become hot, and would not operate; but Mr. Hebert has at last found means to keep it cool. It is one of the most prompt and safe Cannon that ever was invented. It is constructed on a carriage so arranged that it can be

Loaded and Fired while Retreating!

Mr. Hebert will exhibit the Cannon in

CERTIFICATE.

This certifies that the undersigned have examined the model of a Cannon invented by A. Hebert, of the town of Malone, Franklin Co., state of New York. And that we consider it one of the wonders of the age—and that it will be of great utility if adopted into use. And we do not hesitate to say that in our opinion it will bear all competition.

Malone, March 11th, 1862.

NAMES.—O. C. Phelps, Machinist; H. D. Cornish, White Smith; A. Phelps Mechanic; Wm. A. Jones, Grocer; J. H. Hyde, Mechanic; A. S. Walbridge, Machinist; E. M. Cornish, Clerk; Henry Hale, Machinist; James Kennedy, Smith; Godfois Lamvian, Patern Maker R. R. Shop; Wm. B. Earl, Grocer; John Godreau, Machinist; Isaie Guerin, Carpenter; A. H. Davids, Carpenter; Thomas Aubery, R. R. Shops.

Steam Power Presses—Palladium Office—Malone, N. Y.

The Hanes hand grenade, which saw limited use during the War, was detonated when an impact forced one of its many interior percussion caps against its outer shell. The device was so sensitive that it could explode at the slightest jar.

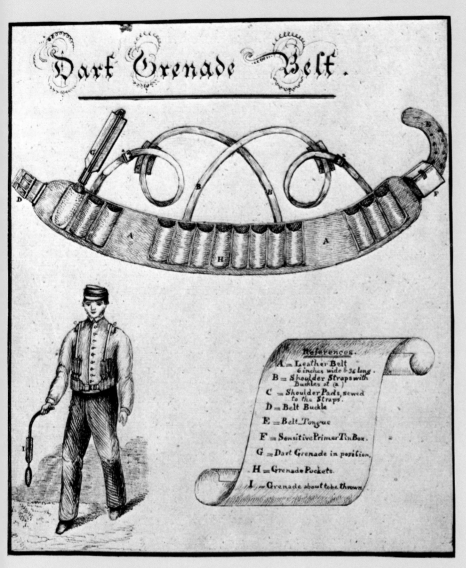

This leather belt was designed by Confederate General Gabriel J. Rains to carry 14 dart grenades. As the figure demonstrates, the miniature missiles were to be launched with the aid of a sling and guided by feathered vanes.

As this Adams hand grenade was thrown, the leather wrist strap was intended to jerk the priming pin from the shell to ignite the fuse. The risk to the thrower was dire — if the pin did not emerge smoothly, the live grenade might land at his feet.

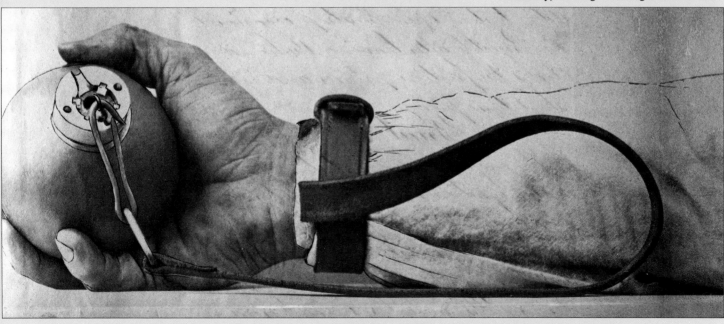

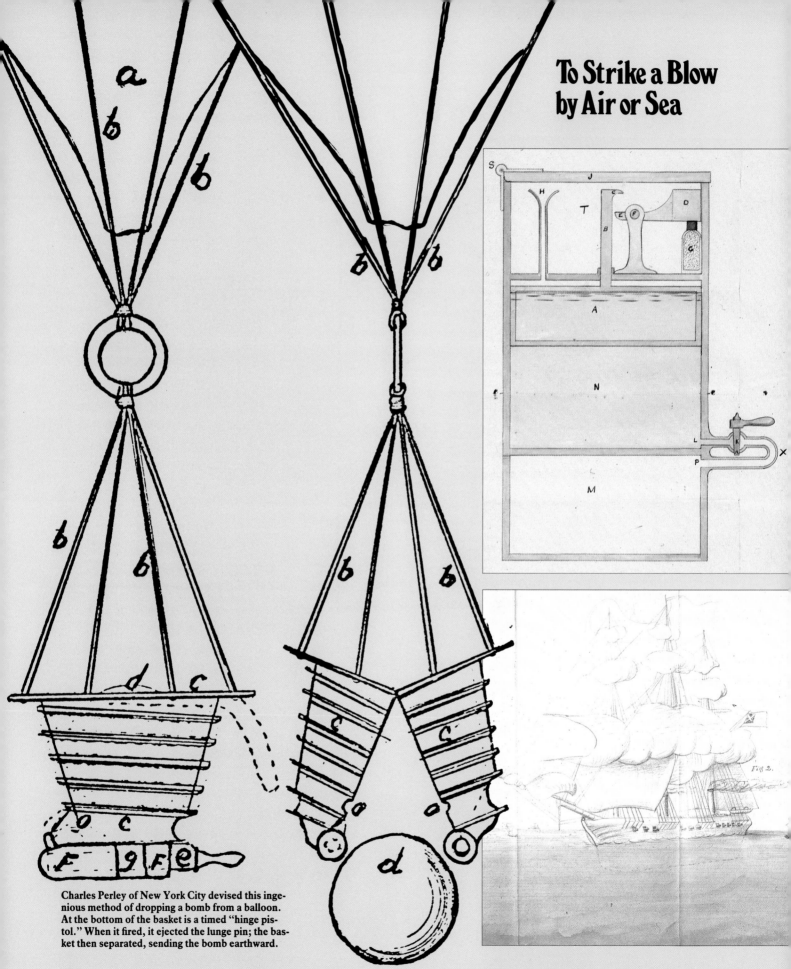

To Strike a Blow
by Air or Sea

Charles Perley of New York City devised this ingenious method of dropping a bomb from a balloon. At the bottom of the basket is a timed "hinge pistol." When it fired, it ejected the lunge pin; the basket then separated, sending the bomb earthward.

164

This self-contained timing mechanism was intended as a safe means of igniting the powder magazines of captured ships or forts. When the stopcock was opened, water would flow into the bottom chamber from the middle one, lowering hook *C* to strike hammer *D*, which in turn detonated grenade *G*.

Another type of aerial bomb, suggested by Lot Wilks of Rockford, Illinois, consisted of a gas-filled balloon separated from a shell by a wooden box. Aloft, a long fuse affixed to the shell burned down and touched off a flash of powder that burst the balloon. Then, as the contraption hurtled to earth, the fuse ignited the shell.

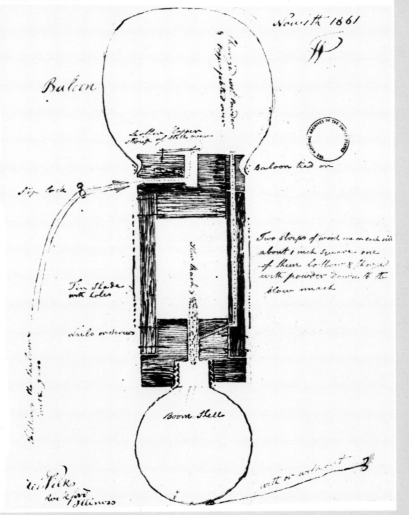

Augustus Stones's submarine torpedo, as shown below, was meant to be guided to an enemy ship from the safety of a Union coastal fort by slender guy wires. The propeller was driven by coiled springs.

Projectiles for the Future

A governor's aide from Davenport, Iowa, named Ira W. Gifford proposed this simple idea for an improved musket ball. When fired, the ball would split like an orange into four sections, causing greater damage on impact.

This futuristic-looking artillery shot was designed and tested by the Confederate ordnance department in the hope of achieving greater accuracy from smoothbore guns. As soon as it left the cannon barrel, the projectile sprouted vanes that were intended to impart a stabilizing spin — the same effect that rifled barrels had on shot.

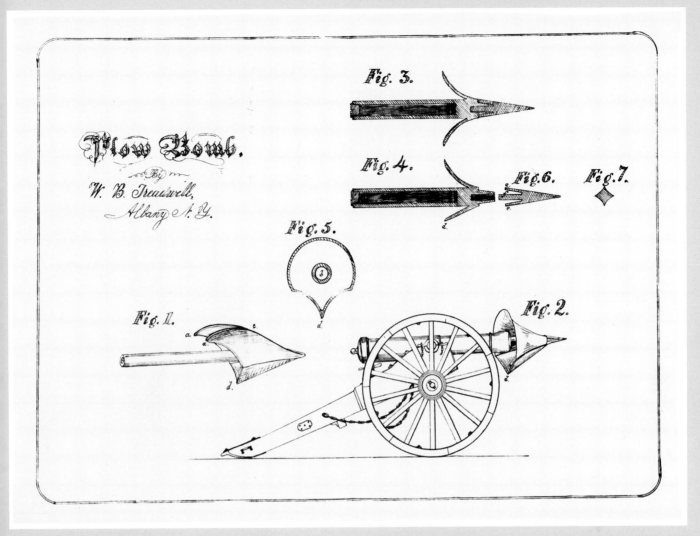

W. B. Treadwell of Albany, New York, predicted that his "Plow Bomb," a spear-headed cannon projectile, would tear apart Confederate earthworks and timber fortifications, but the ordnance office concluded that the weapon's destructive power would be much less than that of the shot and shell in common use.

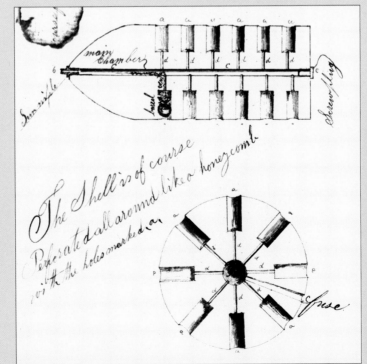

This Pevey shell, shown in halves, was another attempt to add to the lethal effect of artillery projectiles. The inner cavity held powder as usual, but a specially designed outer ring contained a deadly load of iron shot.

Francis Speth of Cincinnati, Ohio, designed an artillery shell honeycombed with short barrels, each containing a ball. On impact, the shell would explode and scatter shot in all directions.

A Search for Deadlier Fire

John D'Arcy of San Francisco wrote that his twin-barreled cannon would "destroy a whole battalion at a single shot." Two cannonballs would be joined by a chain and fired simultaneously, cutting a bloody swath through the Confederate line.

Stephen Bowerman of Battle Creek, Michigan, boasted that the 32 rifle barrels of his "pale horse" could decimate an enemy regiment in five minutes. He made two inquiries to Washington but received only a polite acknowledgment.

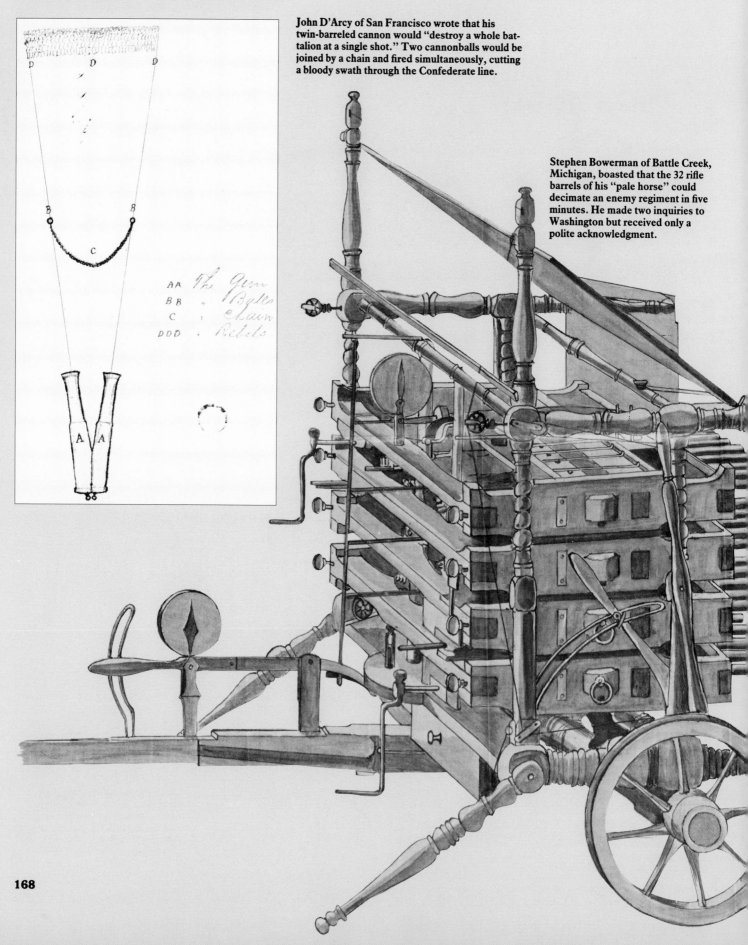

AA The Gun
BB " Byles
C   " Chain
DDD . Rebels

This prototype Gatling gun — the first truly successful rapid-fire weapon — had six barrels that were revolved by a hand crank. Before his death in 1903 Dr. Richard Gatling, the gun's inventor, experimented with an electric motor to power the revolving barrel.

Twenty-five rifle barrels make up the Requia battery, which was briefly used by the Union in the siege at Charleston. The ammunition *(bottom)* was held in place by a strip of brass; the charges were ignited in quick succession — each touched off by the preceding one — like a string of firecrackers.

Ironclad Innovations

A man named Hicks of Grand View, Indiana, devised this formidable-looking "portable breastwork," a huge rolling drum covered with sharp spikes. It was meant to be pushed ahead of advancing troops to protect them from enemy fire while skewering any men or horses in its path.

A correspondent to *Scientific American* magazine designed this infantry shield, meant to protect a column of men from the "tempest of balls, shell or musketry." The device would have been unwieldy at best and useful only on the smoothest terrain. It makes little concession to the fact that, at most ranges, gunfire plunges in from above.

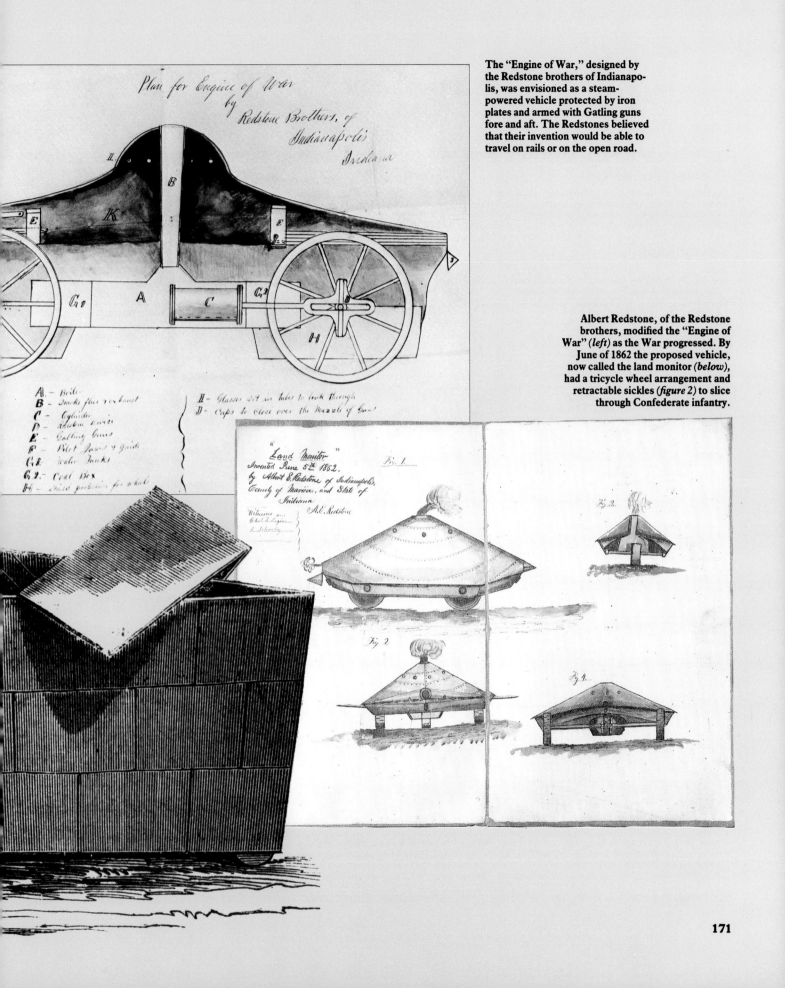

Plan for Engine of War
by
Redstone Brothers, of
Indianapolis
Indiana

A. - Boiler
B. - Smoke flue or exhaust
C. - Cylinder
D. - Steam source
E. - Gatling Guns
F. - Pilot Paws & guide
G.1 - Water Tanks
G.2 - Coal Box
H. - Shield protection for wheel

H - Glasses set in tubes to look through
D - Caps to close over the Muzzle of Guns

"Land Monitor"
Invented June 5th 1862.
by Albert E. Redstone of Indianapolis,
County of Marion, and State of
Indiana.   A.E. Redstone
Witnesses are
Robert R. Lyman
E. Silverby

Fig. 1

Fig. 2

Fig. 3

Fig. 4

The "Engine of War," designed by the Redstone brothers of Indianapolis, was envisioned as a steam-powered vehicle protected by iron plates and armed with Gatling guns fore and aft. The Redstones believed that their invention would be able to travel on rails or on the open road.

Albert Redstone, of the Redstone brothers, modified the "Engine of War" (*left*) as the War progressed. By June of 1862 the proposed vehicle, now called the land monitor (*below*), had a tricycle wheel arrangement and retractable sickles (*figure 2*) to slice through Confederate infantry.

171

ACKNOWLEDGMENTS

The editors thank the following individuals and institutions for their valuable assistance in the preparation of this volume: Connecticut: Waterbury — Frederick W. Chesson. Indiana: Berne — Robert Willey.

Maryland: Baltimore — Erick Davis; Clinton — Bill Turner; Ft. Meade — Earl J. Coates, National Security Agency; New Carrollton — David W. Gaddy. Missouri: Kansas City — Milton F. Perry.

Ohio: Niles — James Frasca.
Washington, D.C.: Dr. Oscar P. Fitzgerald, Navy Memorial Museum; Edward Rich, Smithsonian Institution.
The index was prepared by Roy Nanovic.

BIBLIOGRAPHY

Books

Alexander, E. P., *Military Memoirs of a Confederate*. Dayton: Morningside Bookshop, 1977 (reprint of 1907 edition).

Bakeless, John, *Spies of the Confederacy*. Philadelphia: J. B. Lippincott Co., 1970.

Baker, L. C., *History of the United States Secret Service*. Philadelphia: L. C. Baker, 1867.

Benjamin, L. N., comp., *The St. Albans Raid: or, Investigation into the Charges*. Montreal: John Lovell, 1865.

Beymer, William Gilmore, *On Hazardous Service*. New York: Harper & Brothers, 1912.

Bill, Alfred Hoyt, *The Beleaguered City: Richmond, 1861-1865*. New York: Alfred A. Knopf, 1946.

Bowman, John S., ed., *The Civil War Almanac*. New York: World Almanac Publications, 1983.

Boyd, Belle, *Belle Boyd in Camp and Prison*. Ed. by Curtis Carroll Davis. Cranbury, N.J.: Thomas Yoseloff, 1968.

Branch, John, Sr., comp., *St. Albans Raid*. St. Albans, Vt.: John Branch Sr., 1935.

Brown, George William, *Baltimore and the Nineteenth of April, 1861*. Baltimore: N. Murray, 1887.

Brown, R. Shepard, *Stringfellow of the Fourth*. New York: Crown Publishers, 1960.

Brownlee, Richard S., *Gray Ghosts of the Confederacy*. Baton Rouge: Louisiana State University Press, 1958.

Castel, Albert:
A Frontier State at War: Kansas, 1861-1865. Ithaca, N.Y.: Cornell University Press, 1958.
William Clarke Quantrill: His Life and Times. New York: Frederick Fell, Inc., 1962.

Catton, Bruce:
The Army of the Potomac: Glory Road. Garden City, N.Y.: Doubleday & Co., 1952.
Grant Moves South. Boston: Little, Brown, 1960.
Terrible Swift Sword. Vol. 2. New York: Pocket Books, 1963.

Commager, Henry Steele, ed., *The Blue and the Gray*. New York: The Fairfax Press, 1982.

Connelley, William Elsey, *Quantrill and the Border Wars*. New York: Pageant Book Co., 1956 (reprint of 1909 edition).

Conrad, Thomas N.:
A Confederate Spy. New York: J. S. Ogilvie, 1892.
The Rebel Scout. Washington, D.C.: The National Publishing Co., 1904.

Dowdey, Clifford, *Experiment in Rebellion*. Garden City, N.Y.: Doubleday & Co., 1946.

Dowdey, Clifford, ed., *The Wartime Papers of R. E. Lee*. New York: Bramhall House, 1961.

Dulles, Allen, *The Craft of Intelligence*. New York: Harper and Row, 1967.

Edom, Clifton C., comp. and ed., *Missouri Sketch Book: A Collection of Words and Pictures of the Civil War*. Columbia, Mo.: Lucas Brothers, 1983.

Edwards, John N., *Noted Guerrillas*. St. Louis: Bryan, Brand & Co., 1877.

Emerson, Edward Waldo, *Life and Letters of Charles Russell Lowell*. Boston: Houghton, Mifflin, 1907.

Foote, Shelby, *The Civil War, A Narrative: Fort Sumter to Perryville*. New York: Random House, 1958.

Frassanito, William A., *Antietam*. New York: Charles Scribner's Sons, 1978.

Freeman, Douglas Southall, *Lee's Lieutenants*:
Vol. 2, *Cedar Mountain to Chancellorsville*. New York: Charles Scribner's Sons, 1943.
Vol. 3, *Gettysburg to Appomattox*. New York: Charles Scribner's Sons, 1944.

Hale, Donald R.:
They Called Him Bloody Bill. Clinton, Mo.: The Printery, 1975.
We Rode with Quantrill. Clinton, Mo.: The Printery, 1975.

Haupt, Herman, *Reminiscences of General Herman Haupt*. Milwaukee: Wright & Joys Co., 1901.

Headley, John W., *Confederate Operations in Canada and New York*. New York: The Neale Publishing Co., 1906.

Hesseltine, William B., ed., *Civil War Prisons*. Kent, Ohio: Kent State University Press, 1962.

Hildebrand, Samuel S., *Autobiography of Samuel S. Hildebrand*. Comp. by James W. Evans and A. Wendell Keith. Jefferson City, Mo.: State Times Book and Job Printing House, 1870.

Hirshson, Stanley P., *Grenville M. Dodge*. Bloomington: Indiana University Press, 1967.

Hoadley, John Chipman, *Memorial of Henry Sanford Gansevoort*. Boston: Avery & Co., 1875.

Horan, James D., *Confederate Agent: A Discovery in History*. New York: Crown Publishers, 1954.

Howard, F. K., *Fourteen Months in American Bastiles*. Baltimore: Kelly, Hedian & Piet, 1863.

Humphreys, Charles A., *Field, Camp, Hospital and Prison in the Civil War, 1863-1865*. Freeport, N.Y.: Books for Libraries Press, 1971 (reprint of 1918 edition).

Ingenthron, Elmo, *Borderland Rebellion: A History of the Civil War on the Missouri-Arkansas Border*. Ed. by Kathleen Van Buskirk. Branson, Mo.: The Ozarks Mountaineer, 1980.

Johnson, Robert Underwood, and Clarence Clough Buel, eds., *Battles and Leaders of the Civil War*. Vols. 1 and 3. New York: The Century Co., 1888.

Jones, Virgil Carrington:
Gray Ghosts and Rebel Raiders. New York: Henry Holt and Co., 1956.
Ranger Mosby. Chapel Hill: University of North Carolina Press, 1944.

Kane, Harnett T., *Spies for the Blue and Gray*. New York: Ace Books, 1954.

Kinchen, Oscar A., *Confederate Operations in Canada and the North*. North Quincy, Mass.: The Christopher Publishing House, 1970.

Leech, Margaret, *Reveille in Washington*. TIME Reading Program Special Edition. Alexandria, Va.: Time-Life Books, 1980.

Meredith, Roy, and Arthur Meredith, *Mr. Lincoln's Military Railroads*. New York: W. W. Norton & Co., 1979.

Miller, Francis Trevelyan, ed., *Soldier Life and the Secret Service*. Vol. 8 of *The Photographic History of the Civil War*. New York: The Review of Reviews Co., 1912.

Milton, George Fort, *Abraham Lincoln and the Fifth Column*. New York: The Vanguard Press, 1942.

Mogelever, Jacob, *Death to Traitors*. Garden City, N.Y.: Doubleday & Co., 1960.

Monaghan, Jay:
Civil War on the Western Border: 1854-1865. Boston: Little, Brown, 1955.
Swamp Fox of the Confederacy: The Life and Military Services of M. Jeff Thompson. Tuscaloosa, Ala.: Confederate Publishing Co., 1956.

Monteiro, Aristides, *War Reminiscences by the Surgeon of Mosby's Command*. Richmond: E. Waddey, 1890.

Mosby, John S., *The Memoirs of Colonel John S. Mosby*. Ed. by Charles Wells Russell. Millwood, N.Y.: Kraus Reprint, 1981.

Myer, Albert J., *A Manual of Signals for the Use of Signal Officers in the Field*. New York: D. Van Nostrand, 1868.

Nicolay, John G., *A Short Life of Abraham Lincoln*. New York: The Century Co., 1904.

O'Neill, Charles, *Wild Train*. New York: Random House, 1956.

Patrick, Marsena R., *Inside Lincoln's Army: The Diary of Marsena Rudolph Patrick*. Ed. by David S. Sparks. New York: Thomas Yoseloff, 1964.

Perry, Milton F., *Infernal Machines: The Story of Confederate Submarine and Mine Warfare*. Baton Rouge: Louisiana State University Press, 1965.

Pinkerton, Allan, *The Spy of the Rebellion*. New York: G. W. Dillingham, 1888.

Pittenger, William, *Daring and Suffering: A History of the Great Railroad Adventure*. Philadelphia: J. W. Daughaday, 1863.

Porter, Horace, *Campaigning with Grant*. (Collector's Library of the Civil War series). Alexandria, Va.: Time-Life Books, 1981 (reprint of 1897 edition).

Rowan, Richard Wilmer, *The Story of Secret Service*. New York: The Literary Guild of America, 1937.

Rowan, Richard Wilmer, and Robert G. Deindorfer, *Secret Service: Thirty-Three Centuries of Espionage*. London: William Kimber, 1969.

Sandburg, Carl, *Abraham Lincoln: The War Years*. Vol. 1. New York: Harcourt, Brace & World, 1939.

Sangston, Lawrence, *The Bastiles of the North*. Baltimore: Kelly, Hedian & Piet, 1863.

Sears, Stephen W., *Landscape Turned Red*. New Haven, Conn.: Ticknor & Fields, 1983.

Settle, William A., Jr., *Jesse James Was His Name*. Columbia: University of Missouri Press, 1966.

Siepel, Kevin H., *Rebel: The Life and Times of John Singleton Mosby*. New York: St. Martin's Press, 1983.

Sigaud, Louis A., *Belle Boyd: Confederate Spy*. Richmond: Dietz Press, 1944.

Smith, Henry Bascome, *Between the Lines: Secret Service Stories*. New York: Booz Brothers, 1911.

Starr, Stephen Z., *Jennison's Jayhawkers*. Baton Rouge: Louisiana State University Press, 1973.

Thomas, Benjamin P., and Harold M. Hyman, *Stanton*. New York: Alfred A. Knopf, 1962.

Thompson, Henry C., *Sam Hildebrand Rides Again*. Bonne

Terre, Mo.: Steinbeck, 1950.

Townsend, Thomas S., *Honors of the Empire State in the War of the Rebellion.* New York: A. Lovell and Co., 1889.

Volck, Adalbert Johann, *The Work of Adalbert Johann Volck.* Baltimore: George McCullough Anderson, 1970.

Warner, Ezra J.:
Generals in Blue: Lives of the Union Commanders. Baton Rouge: Louisiana State University Press, 1964.
Generals in Gray: Lives of the Confederate Commanders. Baton Rouge: Louisiana State University Press, 1959.

Williams, Kenneth P., *Iuka to Vicksburg.* Vol. 4 of *Lincoln Finds a General.* New York: Macmillan Co., 1956.

Williamson, James J., *Mosby's Rangers: A Record of the Operations of the Forty-Third Battalion Virginia Cavalry.* New York: Ralph B. Kenyon, 1896.

Other Sources

Beymer, William Gilmore, "Miss Van Lew." *Harper's Monthly Magazine,* June 1911.

Boder, Bartlett, "General Odon Guitar Takes Charge in Saint Joseph." *Museum Graphic,* spring 1958.

Castel, Albert:
"The Guerrilla War." *Civil War Times Illustrated,* October 1974.
"Jim Lane of Kansas." *Civil War Times Illustrated,* April 1973.

Ellis, Garrison, "Tracking the Gray Ghost." *Virginia Country's Civil War.* Vol. 1. 1983.

Fishel, Edwin C., "The Mythology of Civil War Intelligence." *Civil War History,* December 1964.

"The Execution of Williams and Peters." *Harper's Weekly,* July 4, 1863.

Gaddy, David W., "Gray Cloaks and Daggers." *Civil War Times Illustrated,* July 1975.

Hale, Laura Virginia, "Belle Boyd." United Daughters of the Confederacy, Warren Rifles Chapter, no date.

Kirby, Michael Ross, "Partisan and Counterpartisan Activity in Northern Virginia." Unpublished thesis. Athens, Georgia, 1977.

McClelland, Russ, " 'We Were Enemies': Pennsylvanians and Virginia Guerrillas." *Civil War Times Illustrated,* December 1983.

Sears, Stephen W., "The First News Blackout." *American Heritage,* June-July 1985.

Wert, Jeffry D., "In One Deadly Encounter." *Civil War Times Illustrated,* November 1980.

PICTURE CREDITS

Credits from left to right are separated by semicolons, from top to bottom by dashes.

Cover: Painting by Gilbert Gaul, from The Warner Collection of Gulf States Paper Corporation, Tuscaloosa, Ala. 2, 3: Maps by Peter McGinn. 9: Library of Congress. 11: The Kunhardt Collection. 12: Erick Davis Collection (2) — courtesy Frank & Marie-T. Wood Print Collections, Alexandria, Va. 13: The New-York Historical Society, New York City — courtesy Frank & Marie-T. Wood Print Collections, Alexandria, Va. 14-17: Courtesy Frank & Marie-T. Wood Print Collections, Alexandria, Va. 18, 19: Erick Davis Collection. 20: Erick Davis Collection — courtesy Frank & Marie-T. Wood Print Collections, Alexandria, Va. 22: From *The Spy of the Rebellion,* by Allan Pinkerton, published by G. W. Dillingham, New York, 1888. 25: Kean Archives, Philadelphia. 28: Library of Congress. 29: From *The Spy of the Rebellion,* by Allan Pinkerton, published by G. W. Dillingham, New York, 1888. 30: Drawing by Edwin Forbes, Library of Congress — National Archives Neg. No. 165-SB-46. 31: From *Russell's Civil War Photographs: 116 Historic Prints,* by Andrew J. Russell, published by Dover Publications, Inc., New York, 1982. 32, 33: Massachusetts Commandery of the Military Order of the Loyal Legion of the United States/U.S. Army Military History Institute (MASS/MOLLUS/USAMHI), copied by A. Pierce Bounds. 34: From *On Hazardous Service,* by William Gilmore Beymer, published by Harper & Brothers, New York, 1912. 35-43: From *The Spy of the Rebellion,* by Allan Pinkerton, published by G. W. Dillingham, New York, 1888. 45: Museum of the Confederacy, Richmond, photographed by Larry Sherer; Francis Lord Collection, photographed by Harold Norvell. 46: National Archives, Military Archives Division, photographed by Larry Sherer — inset from *Military Memoirs of a Confederate: A Critical Narrative,* by E. P. Alexander, © 1907 by Charles Scribner's Sons, reprint published by Morningside Bookshop, Dayton, Ohio, 1977. 47: Valentine Museum, Richmond. 48: Library of Congress. 49: Alabama State Department of Archives and History, Military Collection; William L. Clements Library, The University of Michigan. 50: From *The Work of Adalbert Johann Volck,* © 1970 by George McCullough Anderson, Baltimore. 53: Rinhart Galleries, courtesy Historical Times Inc. 54: Courtesy Marian B. Ralph, copied by Charles Phillips. 55: Special Collections Department, Carol M. Newman Library, Virginia Polytechnic Institute and State University. 56: Erick Davis Collection. 57: From *History of the United States Secret Service,* by L. C. Baker, Philadelphia, 1867. 58, 59: From *Prisons and Hospitals,* Vol. 7 of *The Photographic History of the Civil War,* edited by Francis Trevelyan Miller, published by The Review of Reviews Co., 1912, insets Chicago Historical Society; John L. McGuire Collection; Library of Congress. 60: St. Albans Historical Society — courtesy Frank & Marie-T. Wood Print Collections, Alexandria, Va. 61: Courtesy Frank & Marie-T. Wood Print Collections, Alexandria, Va. — St. Albans Historical Society. 62: Courtesy Frank & Marie-T. Wood Print Collections, Alexandria, Va. 64: Herb Peck Jr. — National Archives, Military Archives Division, photographed by George Stokes; National Archives, Military Archives Division, photographed by Larry Sherer. 65: National Archives Neg. No. 165-C-571. 66: Cipher wheel courtesy Museum of the Confederacy, Richmond, photographed by Larry Sherer. 67: National Archives, Military Archives Division, photographed by Larry Sherer. 68: Smithsonian Institution, Washington, D.C., photographed by Peter Harholt — Library of Congress. 69: Library of Congress, inset Smithsonian Institution, Washington, D.C., photographed by Peter Harholt. 70: National Archives, Military Archives Division, photographed by George Stokes. 71: Coded telegraph message, National Archives, Military Archives Division, photographed by Larry Sherer — plain-text message by Harris Andrews, adapted from the original in the National Archives. 73: National Archives, Military Archives Division, photographed by Larry Sherer. 74: National Archives Neg. No. 111-B-2748. 76, 77: Courtesy Frank & Marie-T. Wood Print Collections, Alexandria, Va. 79: Museum of the Confederacy, Richmond, photographed by Larry Sherer. 80: MASS/MOLLUS/USAMHI, copied by A. Pierce Bounds. 82, 83: Library of Congress. 84, 85: Drawing by Alfred R. Waud, Library of Congress — Kean Archives, Philadelphia. 87: Valentine Museum, Richmond. 88: From *On Hazardous Service,* by William Gilmore Beymer, published by Harper & Brothers, New York, 1912. 90, 91: National Archives Neg. Nos. 77-F-194-6-54; 77-F-194-6-53. 92, 93: Library of Congress. 94, 95: Library of Congress; National Archives Neg. No. 77-F-194-6-51. 96, 97: Library of Congress; National Archives Neg. No. 77-F-194-6-57. 98, 99: National Archives Neg. No. 111-B-505. 100: National Archives Neg. Nos. 111-B-6169 — 111-B-397. 101: Library of Congress. 102, 103: National Archives Neg. No. 77-F-194-6-63; Library of Congress. 104: Special Collections (Orlando Poe Collection), U.S. Military Academy Library, West Point, New York, copied by Henry Groskinsky — Library of Congress. 105: Library of Congress. 107: Painting by W. D. Washington, courtesy Museum of the Confederacy, Richmond, photographed by Larry Sherer. 108: Erick Davis Collection. 109: Museum of the Confederacy, Richmond, copied by Larry Sherer. 111: Map by William L. Hezlep — West Point Museum Collections, U.S. Military Academy, photographed by Henry Groskinsky — from *In Pursuit of the General: A History of the Civil War Railroad Raid,* by William Pittenger, © 1965 by Golden West Books, San Marino, Calif. 112, 113: Drawings by Walton Taber, American Heritage Picture Collection. 114: Courtesy Bill Turner. 117: Erick Davis Collection. 118, 119: National Archives Neg. No. 111-B-5190. 120, 121: Library of Congress except top right MASS/MOLLUS/USAMHI, copied by A. Pierce Bounds. 122, 123: Courtesy Brian Pohanka; National Archives Neg. No. 111-B-6332. 125: Sketch by James E. Taylor, courtesy The Western Reserve Historical Society, Cleveland, Ohio. 128, 129: Painting by Armand Dumaresq, courtesy Museum of the Confederacy, Richmond, photographed by Larry Sherer. 130, 131: Painting by John J. Porter, courtesy Beverly Mosby Coleman, photographed by Larry Sherer. 132: From *Mosby's Rangers,* by James J. Williamson, published by Ralph B. Kenyon, New York, 1896. 133: The Mainfort Collection. 134: Museum of the Confederacy, Richmond, copied by Larry Sherer. 135: MASS/MOLLUS/USAMHI, copied by A. Pierce Bounds. 136: Virginia State Library. 137: Valentine Museum, Richmond. 138: Courtesy Bill Turner. 139: Valentine Museum, Richmond. 141: From *Stories of Missouri,* by John Roy Musick, published by American Book Company, New York, 1897, courtesy Jackson County Historical Society, Independence, Mo. 143: Baker Collection, on loan to Tennessee State Museum, Nashville, photographed by Bill LaFevor — Thomas J. Evans Collection, courtesy *THE KEPI Magazine.* 145: Library of Congress. 146, 147: From *The Work of Adalbert Johann Volck,* © 1970 by George McCullough Anderson, Baltimore; The Kansas State Historical Society, Topeka. 148: Ohio Historical Society, photographed by David R. Barker — George Hart Collection. 150: Civil War Photo Album, Special Collections, Manuscripts and Archives, Louisiana State University Libraries; Tilghman Collection, Western History Collections, University of Oklahoma Library — Dr. Thomas P. Sweeney; Martin Ismert Collection, courtesy Historical Society of Missouri. 151: Jackson County Historical Society, Independence, Mo.; The State Historical Society of Missouri — Dr. Thomas P. Sweeney; George Hart Collection. 154: Courtesy Frank & Marie-T. Wood Print Collections, Alexandria, Va. 155: Littlejohn Collection. 156, 157: Painting by George Caleb Bingham, courtesy Cincinnati Art Museum, The Edwin and Virginia Irwin Memorial, Acc. No. 1958.515. 158: The Kansas State Historical Society, Topeka. 159: National Archives Neg. No. 111-B-1789. 160: The State Historical Society of Missouri. 162: National Archives, Military Archives Division, photographed by Larry Sherer — courtesy Ralph V. Righton, photographed by Michael W. Thomas. 163: Museum of the Confederacy, Richmond, photographed by Larry Sherer — National Archives Record Group 156, Entry 201, Vol. 6, page 290. 164, 165: From *Civil War Times Illustrated*,

February 1975, published by Historical Times Inc., Harrisburg, Pa. (2); National Archives, Military Archives Division, photographed by Larry Sherer (3). 166: National Archives, Military Archives Division, photographed by Larry Sherer — courtesy Thomas S. Dickey, photographed by Michael W. Thomas — National Archives, Record Group 156, Entry 201, Vol. 6, page 318. 167: National Archives, Military Archives

Division, photographed by Larry Sherer. 168, 169: National Archives, Military Archives Division, photographed by Larry Sherer (2); Navy Memorial Museum, photographed by Steve Biver — National Archives, Record Group 156, Entry 201, Vol. 21, page 64. 170, 171: National Archives, Military Archives Division, photographed by Larry Sherer, except bottom left Library of Congress.

INDEX